PATHS AS YET UNTRODDEN

A Journey of Faith and Hope

Except where otherwise indicated, scripture quotations are from The Holy Bible, New International Version

Copyright 1973, 1978, 1984

International Bible Society,

Used by permission

INTRODUCTION

I have adapted some words from a prayer for the title of this book. It is a prayer in the Lutheran Book of Worship (Augsburg, 1978) known as A Prayer for Courage, and it says:

- Lord God, You have called your servants to ventures of which we cannot see the ending, by paths as yet untrodden, through perils unknown. Give us faith to go out with good courage, not knowing where we go, but only that your hand is leading us and your love supporting us. Through Jesus Christ our Lord. Amen.

The prayer was actually written by Eric Milner-White (1884 – 1963) a British Anglican priest, academic, and a decorated military chaplain who included it in his "Daily Prayer" of 1941 and1959. It was first picked up and used in a Lutheran Hymnal in 1958 and today it is used by many groups, as a prayer for courage.

I did not know it until I heard it for the first time in the winter of 2016 as a post communion prayer at the Holy Trinity Lutheran church n Buffalo, where I sojourned for three months while waiting for a copy of my baptismal certificate to be sent from Tanzania. What I'm calling a sojourn came after my much anticipated journey from Cincinnati to Toronto came abruptly to an end. I felt in my heart that the prayer was written for me and my situation.

All that I knew at that time was that it was going to be a matter of a short time and I'd be on my way to Toronto. September 2017 marked the second anniversary of the beginning of my journey. I am now in Washington DC still confident it will be only a short while and I'll be on my way to Toronto.

When I reflect on this sojourn, I am led to look at my experience in the last seven years, for I would not have been on this journey but for the reality in the seven years. The facts surrounding my situation and experience speak for themselves. There is no doubt that the whole experience is a life on the precipice. Indeed when I decided to write this book I debated with myself whether to have "Life on the Precipice" as the title or make the the prayer the title.

When we prayed this prayer at the Holy Trinity Lutheran Church it reminded me of the Israelites' 40 years sojourn in the desert on the way to the promised land. It reminded me of what emotions Abraham must have felt in his dealings with God and the implications of that experience. It reminded me of not only Abraham but the patriarchs and matriarchs. Theirs was a story of uncertainty yet filled with hope – I hope.

That is how I got to think of these past seven years. This was a period that, because of the situation I was in – which ultimately informed me of the necessity to move on – I lived on the precipice. It was a period of more uncertainties than assurances. I did not have security in terms of work and income or health. But I also could echo St. Paul's words to the Christians in Corinth: "Hard pressed on every side, but not crushed; perplexed, but not in despair; persecuted, but not abandoned; struck down, but not destroyed" (2 Cor. 4: 8-9).

This period has also brought back memories of the time I lived in Israel and travelled extensively throughout the Holy Land. A reflection on how life is adapted to the terrain gives a better perspective of life and situations or circumstances.

I think of the Beduin shepherds and their goats, sheep and camels in the Judean Desert. I think of the wild goat or ibex, gazelles and Arabian leopards in Ein Gedi. I think of the Griffton vultures, the Nubian ibex and the Sand Cats of Timna and the Negev. Along with thriving plant and insect life that the seemingly desolate landscape supports, I am able to see hope in living on the precipice.

The late long-time Benedictine archaeologist at the Dormitian Abbey on Mount Zion, Bargil Pixner wrote a book, With Jesus Through Galilee: According to the Fifth Gospel, in which he points out that the Holy Land opens up the world of the Bible.

The biggest lesson in all this is that life on the precipice is a shared experience. During this period, I was volunteered in outreach ministry for a faith-based non-profit organization. I was a volunteer chaplain in a Christian health center whose mission is people living on the precipice. I devoted the time to issues of social justice and advocacy. I know I got more out of this experience than I gave.

The second lesson from this experience is the power available in inner fortitude which far exceeds any burden of living on the precipice. I am still learning this source of what some call authentic power, and which I'll refer to as true power, grounded in these six spiritual principles: Hope, Faith, Abundance/Connections, Perseverance, Gratitude, Humility.

Ultimately then, I settled on "Paths Yet Untrodden" for the title because the journey is not over yet – it never ends while we are on this earth – and still, there are no certainties nor fool-proof blueprints. That is why I need hope, faith, perseverance, gratitude, humility, and the acknowledgement of abundance in this life.

It is all about perspective. There is life on the precipice on the one hand, and there is far greater authentic power on the other; and I choose to focus on the latter.

As I acknowledge abundance and connections, I am indebted to many individuals. It will be impossible to mention all of them.. Nevertheless, those who have believed in me and my story, deserve very special mention: Sherman Bradley, Roger Howell, Steve Gerdsen, Keith Vath, Drew Brown, Cary Umhau, Carl Harbour, Kathy Mank and Barbara Rohrer.

This has been shared experience with many, by choice for some, and by Providence, for others. I want to thank all the bible study groups I have been blessed to be part of, especially the men's at Christ Church Cathedral, the Tuesday morning group at Holy Trinity Lutheran Church in Buffalo, and the Wednesdays group at St. Mark's Episcopal Church, Capitol Hill.

You have all made my journey worthwhile and added humanity to my story.

Patience and Perseverance

It has been a long journey with many twists and turns, many of which I could not have prepared for. I keep reminding myself to be calm and pray on. This is advice that came to me from a coffee mug in a government office.

It was mid-afternoon on Friday and I had been sitting in the waiting room of the government agency since 8 in the morning. There were around 150 of us waiting for interview for various services; and there was a constant stream of people coming in and waiting as the hours went by and few leaving. A staff member tried to calm down jittery clients reminding us that we were simply far more than their number could handle expeditiously.

We were given numbers, categorized by a preceding letter – A, B, C, M, R, S, D, Z – which must have meant something to the staff but not to us – and followed by digits. Mine was A028.

There were also computer monitors on the walls which displayed numbers as they were called for interview and also pending to be called. I kept checking the monitor and listening for calls and I sensed that A's had not being called for a while.

I was becoming impatient and thinking of quitting and return on Monday morning. Actually I was there the day before too and it was about the time I had quit when my number was far down on the pending list. Just before I rose to leave, a door opened, a staff personnel appeared. There was dead silence in the waiting room as eyes turned to her eager to hear who she would call.

"Number A-021!" she called. There was silence for about five seconds, then someone shouted, "Gone!" "Twenty-two?" Again, silence, then the whole waiting room responded, "Gone!" She went on, twenty-three, twenty-four, twenty-five, twenty-six, twenty-seven…and the response was the same. Then, "twenty-eight!". I was worried I might not respond quickly enough before the crowd would roar, "gone", so I raised my paperwork above my head and stood up instantly. The crowd roared, "Bingo!".

My patience paid off. I was happy and so were my fellow clients. Actually, I sometimes boast that patience is one of my blessings. But it is not easy. I have to continue learning each day.

I was tempted to blame myself for not being patient the previous day. But I knew I should not blame myself or anyone, nor regret because I acted to the best of the information and knowledge available at that time. Acceptance is the way to happiness.

The officer gestured to a seat in front of her desk while she opened drawers in search of stationery. I noticed, right in front of me, a conspicuous coffee mug that served as a pencil holder, with bright color patterns, and the inscription: "Be calm and pray on".

Why wasn't this mug in the waiting room for all of us to see? I asked myself. But then, I still wonder, would it have made any difference? Are we not, perhaps, reminded in different ways, of the need for patience but we fail to notice and heed?

Abundance

Ideally we prepare, or we are prepared for what we want to be in life. We have heard, for example, how a person is, or is not prepared to be president! It is, indeed the reason, or at least one of the reasons some spend many years training for those tasks they plan to be involved in in their life.

Growing up, I wanted to be a journalist. And journalism in my growing up meant news reporting. Yet, it wasn't news that attracted my interest. Deep down, I was interested in traveling the world. I spent hours looking at postcards and geography books of New Zealand, Switzerland, Argentina and so on. I even developed interest in drawing and painting landscapes; green valleys and snow covered mountains and thick forests of Germany.

In Secondary School that changed. Not the desire for world travel but the means.

When I went to secondary school we had emerged from colonial rule only a few years earlier. So, we still had a lot of vestiges of colonial practices and especially in mindset.

One of them was privilege. Those who made it in the school system had assurances of a career and the requisite training. So. In secondary school we had a careers master, one of the academic staff who guided us in choosing a career.

Up to 12th grade my choice was journalism. But then, just weeks before we submitted our final choices, some brochures and application materials arrived from the ministry of finance for training of future accountants. Selected candidates would be trained in one of these Commonwealth countries: England, Canada, Australia or New Zealand. There was my incentive – right there. Now there was that certainty of my favorite countries. In journalism there was a possibility, may be even a strong probability. In accounting there was assurance.

In many ways my class choices pointed to journalism. I dropped Physics and Chemistry and studied history and English literature. I found Physics and Chemistry rather tough for me and was not ready to struggle for them. I did not find the mandatory classes (compulsory as we called it in our English) as intimidating. Actually I liked Biology, Geography and, except for Geometry, I generally enjoyed Mathematics.

So, I truly was prepared to choose journalism for my career. But the enticement of training in a Commonwealth country was too strong. I chose accounting for first choice and journalism for second. The career master recommended me for the second choice but because the government's need for accountants was greater than the need for journalists, I was selected to follow a career in accounting.

I still remember verbatim what the career master wrote for my testimonial.

"Joel can do really well, especially in things that strongly interest him. He has an independent outlook, and although this led to difficulties in a regimented school system, it should prove an asset in his career".

Yes, he was absolutely right. My independent disposition got me into some trouble in boarding schools which require conformity.

In spite of all this though, I did not go to those Commonwealth countries but   went to Nairobi, Kenya (although a Commonwealth country) for initial two-year training and when it was time to go to England for the remaining part of the training I dropped out. Neither have I pursued journalism as a career.

Growing up my parents were very proud of me. My mother especially, always had some very encouraging things to say about me. "You will go to Achimota", she would say, although sometimes she was sarcastic. Achimota College was a prestigious elite secondary school for boys in what is today Ghana but its reputation extended beyond West Africa.

My mother's accolades echoed my primary school headteacher whose words – every time I gave a correct answer in class – were: "All the way to Makerere". Again, Makerere was the premier university in Kampala, Uganda, the cradle of Africa at that time. These compliments were the result of my outstanding academic gifts. My parents valued education, especially my mother who also came from a family that excelled in education.

But the reason I became my parents' pride was my older brother suddenly dropping out of middle school. He was away from home in boarding school when my parents received official notification that he had disappeared from school and nobody knew of his whereabouts. It wasn't long though that he came back home after a brief stay with our maternal grandfather and uncles. Obviously he was not quite welcome in that family that valued education above everything else.

He was named Mashauri, in Swahili, not a very common name but in those days some parents gave their kids names that related to some experience or situation they (parents) might have encounterd. Strangely, Mashauri means troubles, especially court cases. We never learned why my parents picked the name for him. But, later in life, he indeed endured a lot of troubles, beginning with that truancy from school.

In any case, he came home and was determined not to go back to school. So it was my turn to carry on the mantle.

In those days most parents did not value, much less support girls' education. Girls were expected to get married and start their own families. But not my parents, especially my father. They sent my older sister off to a boarding girls middle school and that was very unusual in those days.

With this level of moral support there was pressure to excel, and I did academically. What I found lacking was material support. In secondary school especially, at the beginning of a new semester, most students came back from break with adequate money, some with a lot of it, to carry them through the semester. I hardly had any. I don't know if that is why throughout most of my life I have not seen myself with enough money.

Education was state funded from primary school to university for anyone who made it academically through the government schools. I was one of them. And with that there was always the assurance of placement into the elite of society.

When Julius Nyerere, the first president of Tanzania, and parliament mandated that two years of national service would be required of everyone who benefited from this free education, prospective graduates from various institutions in Dar es Salaam organized a protest march to the State House to voice their opposition. Looking back I now see this mentality of entitlement.

The students read out their grievances, concluding with a rebuke that colonial days were better than this time of self-rule. For a president whose life was dedicated to fighting colonial rule, the statement was an insult. But then, as it often happens, there is always the temptation to see privilege as a right.

In a speech some time later, Nyerere stressed the importance of sacrifice and its implications to the beneficiaries of the sacrifice. Part of that speech was framed and hang in our school library at Old Moshi secondary school. It read as follows:

"Those who receive this privilege therefore have a duty. It is like a man who has been given all the food available in a starving village in order to go to a distant place to bring back supplies. If he takes the food but fails to return with supplies, he is a traitor. Similarly our young men and women who receive education have a duty to repay the sacrifice that others have made".

Many of us committed that part of the speech to memory and I still remember it verbatim half a century later.

Then from there I went to Strathmore College in Nairobi; Swedish Theological Institute; and Hebrew University in Jerusalem; Yale Divinity School and Hebrew Union College. All of this is privilege and certainly, abundance..

One day I was sitting in a popular neighborhood bar, and sharing a conversation about writing with a young lady sitting next to me It was a popular meeting place for people of different backgrounds. Parish missioners also visited and even church groups held annual gatherings there, for various purposes.

Innovative entrepreneurs and aspiring artists and writers found it a source of inspiration and ideas for their projects.

So, the young lady and I were talking about writing. I have always wanted to be a writer and here was someone we shared the same aspiration. She had asked me about my background and I was in the middle of my response when suddenly she said, "That is the other thing!" I had no idea what the other thing was, so I was left starring at her. "That is the other thing", she repeated. "Yale! Yale is not normal. It is not normal for Americans to go to Yale. And here you see foreigners talk about studying at Yale like it is a very normal thing"

I got the point. In fact I remembered hearing something similar when I informed some friends at the Lutheran Church of the Redeemer in Jerusalem that the following Fall I would be going to Yale Divinity School. One of those friends was the director of the Jerusalem YMCA, and he was from Pennsylvania.

"Well, you know what that means, don't you?"

Truthfully, I didn't know at that time, only later. But he said, "Going to Yale gives you a ticket to a secure future". It was a reminder of growing up with promises of security and assurance.

But I had also learned about struggles by the time my friend was making his observations at the narthex of the church that Sunday morning. Actually I was already thinking about the next day, Monday morning when I would join a fellow student from the Hebrew University to scale a residential high rise to secure white slabs to the walls of the building to enhance the distinctive white color of Jerusalem architecture. Ironically, my friend lived in one of those high rises where we worked.

This kind of struggle for graduate students abroad was not known back in Tanzania. There was an assumption of smooth sailing in studies overseas. After all, that was the mindset when we were growing up - privilege. I remember the suspicion we felt one day when the bishop in our diocese recounted how he "dug roads" in the summer when he was a graduate student in Minneapolis. "Tulichimba mabarabara", "we dag roads", meaning construction work in general.

And there I was, "chimba mabarabara" to supplement my studies in Jerusalem. But that was the closest I got to actual construction work. I found part-time work washing cars and mopping floors for families before Shabbat.

It began one day when I responded to an advertisement in a local paper for part-time help and no specifics. I was open for whatever I could do to earn regular income. It was still summer and some friends who had promised to help were still out of the country.

The lady who posted the ad in the newspaper arranged to meet with me at Notre Dame Center. She picked me up at the appointed time and took me to her house in Talpiot and showed me the work for which she needed help. It would be on Fridays, early evening before the beginning of Shabbat, washing her car, mopping the floor and raking the lawn all around the house.

Nothing difficult and eventually she introduced me to a neighbor and before I knew it the whole neighborhood had a chore for me on a part time basis. But then when my priest friend at Notre Dame learned of my steadily increasing clientele he brought up the privilege card: "Surely that is not for you", he pointed out. I took his advice and gave up my cleaning contracts.

As a seminarian in Tanzania, during my internship year, I got a chance to study at the Swedish Theological Institute in Jerusalem in the Spring. For the first time, Swedish Theological Institute opened the spring semester for international students. There were eleven of us, one from Taiwan, one from Pakistan, two from India, two from Namibia, one from Zimbabwe, two from Sweden, one from Iceland, and me, from Tanzania.

There are quite a few Jewish holidays in the spring and so our study in Jerusalem included the Exodus Motif, Rabbinic Literature, History of the Second Temple Period, Eastern Christianity, Archaeology and of course, Jewish-Christian Relations, the mission of the Swedish Theological Institute.

This could be a whole topic of another book, but I am relating it here briefly in connection with building connections.

For me especially, coming from Tanzania where, to my knowledge, there were no Jews living in Tanzania – difficult as it is to imagine anywhere where there are no Jews – which could make for a subject of a joke – the experience was an eye-opener. I had never seen a Jew. As a matter of fact, like most Africans at that time, we knew Jews only in reference to the Old Testament. Who even thought of modern secular Jews and a modern religion with no temple sacrifices?

The semester at the Swedish Theological Institute was in the Spring, so one major course was the Exodus Motif which covered the Passover in the book of Exodus and its celebration today in the Seder Meal. For that celebration each one of us was a guest in a Jewish home where we participated in the Passover Haggadah. It was this experience that made me change the topic of my B.D thesis at the seminary to The Last Supper as a Jewish Seder Meal.

As part of this course we also spent a week in the Sinai Desert which was still controlled by Israel. Indeed, we were most probably the last pilgrims to Sinai under Israeli control as it was returned to Egyptian control thereafter.

We spent the week sleeping in sleeping bags, a shocking experience for my fellow Africans in the group. They thought it was too much hardship, that we did not travel all the way from Africa to sleep in sleeping bags in a desert. I enjoyed the experience, and so did the rest of the group, but out of sensitivity for the three other Africans we cut the trip short and returned to Jerusalem.

We also celebrated Purim, another Spring festival derived from the book of Esther but not commanded in the bible. For some Christians the requirement in the Talmud to drink more wine on this celebration than one normally drinks was an eye-opener of sorts. Especially since one must not only drink but must get drunk to the point of being unable to distinguish between "cursed be Haman" and "blessed be Mordechai".

On a more serious note my favorite course was History of the Second Temple Period which included a study of the Dead Sea Scrolls. Even though in seminary we talked of an Intertestamental Period, we still had this idea of a break between the Old Testament era and the New Testament and a period of silence from God.

As a matter of fact, there are preachers who speak of 400 years of silence – I heard that recently – when no word, no communication came forth from God. The course was quite an opener to this period of the emergence of sectarians and varieties of Judaism, a period of tremendous activity. This helps us understand better the emergence of the Jesus movement.

This course provided the foundation for my S.T.M thesis at Yale Divinity School on the Pharisees and their role in preserving and shaping post- 70 A.D Judaism, and also how to better understand the New Testament and its portrayal of animosity between Jesus and the Pharisees.

I developed keen interest in Jewish-Christian Relations as a result of this exposure and interaction with the land and the people of Israel. Both my thesis for B.D and S.T.M were directly the result of a new mindset. I was beginning to appreciate the connection between Judaism and the beginning of Christianity.

At the end of the semester I made arrangements to spend three months in a kibbutz as a volunteer. I thought living in a kibbutz would advance my modern Hebrew but the effort failed.

As it turned out the local residents, most of them immigrants from North Africa and Italy were also interested in improving their English. Nevertheless, the experience was worthwhile in a lot of ways.

My interest in the land of Israel and its people and Jewish-Christian relations led to more connections: I was one of the members in the first-ever conference between Jewish scholars and African theologians on African soil, held in Nairobi. I went on to the XII conference of the International Organization for the Study of the Old Testament in Jerusalem where I reconnected with most of the participants of the Nairobi symposium.

By this time my contacts had reached the highest levels of the World Jewish Congress in Geneva as well as prominent academics in Israel. Through these contacts I was able to study for a year at the Rothberg School for International Students and later graduate studies in Comparative Religion at the Hebrew University of Jerusalem.

During a conference in Jerusalem to mark the 40th anniversary of the discovery of the Dead Sea Scrolls, my circle of contacts was widening. Indeed it was during that conference that I met the then president of Hebrew Union College who extended an invitation for me to pursue graduate studies at the college in Cincinnati.

Though I did not think much, if at all, about the invitation at that time, four years later I enrolled into the Ph.D program at Hebrew Union College.

Feeling Connected is a Basic Human Need

So, I am in Washington. September 16 was the second anniversary of my departure from Cincinnati on a journey to Toronto.

One Sunday morning I went to church at St. Margaret's Episcopal Church. Actually it was the third Sunday I was there because the first time I was simply curious what kind of congregation it would be. I had heard about it, plus I have tried to visit different churches.

There is something in the Episcopal liturgy that made me fall in love with the Episcopal church. Of course another beauty of the Episcopal church is the different practices within its parishes – diversity, in every sense of the word. So, some

Sundays I've gone to an Anglo-Catholic parish where the whole Mass is chanted and the presiding priest is assisted by a deacon and a sub-deacon. I still wonder who a sub-deacon is.

But the whole experience gives a medieval feeling to it, with incense, kneeling and genuflecting at appropriate times during the liturgy. And it is all a dimension of the arts, bringing all the five senses to the worship experience.

Although I am analytical in disposition, I am more inclined to the right side of the brain. I enjoy music, especially classical and church music. There is in my heart and mind love for the pipe organ, appropriately designated by some as the instrument of all instruments.

Then I've been to St. Mark's Episcopal Church on Capitol Hill, a founding member of Progressive Christianity, where ,on my very first Sunday, the First Reading was a poem by the Chilean poet, Pablo Neruda rather than the lectionary designated reading from the Hebrew bible. The whole service is informal but within the Episcopal liturgy.

What attracted me to St. Mark's in general is the Sermon Seminar, where the sermon in the first service is replaced with a sermon and discussion between the first and second service. As many visitors have noted, during the sermon seminar you get to experience how extremely articulate the people at St. Mark's are.

I was also attracted by the variety of small groups that make community tangible, practical and personal at St. Mark's. On my first weekend there I attended a Third Agers (people over 60) presentation where a former obituaries editor of the Washington Post talked about the benefits and techniques of, if not actually writing your own obituary, at least intimating to whoever will write it what you would want to be included in it.

One of the several bible study groups at St. Mark's became my home group, and I'll have more about that later.

It was still in my journey of discovery when I came to St. Margaret's, a liberal parish somewhere between Ascension and St. Agnes on the one end and St. Mark's on Capitol Hill on the other. As always, the liturgy at St. Margaret's, in all its beauty inspires the spirit. I must confess that I find inspiration even in the clerical vestments in the liturgy, something I grew up with.

Anyway, it was during fellowship hour after church at St. Margaret's that after an extended conversation with one of the parishioners I stated that in spite of the long time I have been "stranded" in Washington, my mind is still focused on Toronto. At the end of our conversation she said, "well, I wish you all the best with your plans for Toronto, but on the other hand I'm glad you are stranded in Washington".

One piece of advice I got from one of my best friends in Cincinnati when my journey abruptly halted at Niagara Falls was to not retreat to Cincinnati as some of my other friends were urging me to do because I already had connections there. My friend's advice was, "you are capable of making connections anywhere especially Washington DC".

Indeed, I have been blessed with connections at all times in my life, and certainly, Washington DC is ideal for connections even if you are not a lobbyist. Actually I can say I fell in love with Washington within only a few days of my arrival. Those who don't know Washington have pictures in mind of a place where nothing happens, a center of gridlock. But nothing is further from the truth.

In my first week in Washington I got connected, through a church, with Washington Interfaith Network a grassroots organization committed to addressing various aspects of community issues. Even before I knew the neighborhoods, I was already knocking doors to invite residents to participate in influencing desired developments in their community. I particularly enjoyed seeing an elected representative standing before the assembly and promising, point by point, to push for implementation of the assembly's stated desires. It was y first experience where citizen advocacy groups call in elected officials to declare publicly their commitment to push for citizens' issues.

I will have more to say about intentional connections later but the remark by the sweet lady at St. Margaret's is not isolated. I have been asked many times, "are you still going to Toronto?" to which I have responded with strong affirmation. The people who have asked have given me unmistakable impression that they would be happy if I stayed. And it has been tempting to imagine Washington as my destination.

But that is not why I left Cincinnati, and my status in Washington is not different from what it was in Cincinnati. But, even more important is the final goal and my unwavering commitment to the goal.

Hope is a big part of my life. I am a hopeful optimistic individual. There are three elements of hope. One is a goal. My goal of going to Toronto has been built on the generally accepted view of Toronto as an international and diverse city and Canadian society as representative of inclusion, diversity and welcoming. The so-called American dream is now to be found in Canada. The world now looks to Canada.

The second element of hope is agency or the means to carry the plan forward. It is the commitment to do what it takes to attain the goal. In this is also the willingness to adjust as circumstances make it necessary and the ability to adapt or articulate the goal to any new circumstances. Adjustment and adaptation do not mean retreat. Actually, new connections are an important element in adjustment and adaptation.

The third element of hope is the ability to persevere or to persist. We can also call it tenacity, the spirit to hang on no matter what. Preachers like to remind people in transition, those in the middle, that it is not your destination. However difficult the situation, it is only a point between A and B.

That has always been my message too to people in recovery or those facing any sort of adversity. I remind everyone of St. Paul's advice: "I press on toward the goal to win the prize for which God has called me heavenward in Jesus Christ" (Philippians 3: 14). Actually this is one of my favorite bible verses.

I don't know how many times I have heard this adaptation of Ecclesiastes 9: 11 and Hebrews 12: 1, "the race is not given to the swift but to the one who can endure". This is given to encourage perseverance when in affliction. The actual quote in Ecclesiastes 9: 11 says, "...The race is not to the swift or the battle to the strong, nor does food come to the wise or wealth to the brilliant or favor to the learned; but time and chance happen to them all". And in Hebrews 12: 1 we are told this: "Therefore, since we are surrounded by such a great cloud of witnesses, let us throw off everything that hinders and the sin that so easily entangles. And let us run with perseverance the race marked out for us".

The keyword here is perseverance. In my Romans class for men in recovery I paid very special emphasis on Romans 5: 1-5 because of the combination of some of the attributes I discuss in this book. Paul writes, "Therefore, since we have been justified through faith, we have peace with God through our Lord Jesus Christ through whom we have gained access by faith into this grace in which we now stand. And we boast in the hope of the glory of God. Not only so, but we also glory in our suffering, because we know that suffering produces perseverance; perseverance character; character hope. And hope does not put us to shame". Some translations say "hope does not disappoint us".

I insisted that they underline and pay special attention to the relationship between these terms in the passage: Justification, faith, peace, grace, hope, suffering, perseverance, character, shame (actually lack of shame and disappointment).

When we embark on a journey like mine, physical and spiritual, often we have nothing to hang on to except faith. And faith is not at all easy or free of obstacles and setbacks, otherwise it would not be faith. How else would I completely trust God if there were no obstacles, or situations and circumstances to contend with? Those are the very elements that highlight faith.

As a matter of fact, my principal prayer from which I got the title for this book includes in its petition the fact that we are called "to ventures of which we cannot see the ending, by paths as yet untrodden, through perils unknown".

There is recognition that there may be more unknowns than knowns, more uncertainties than assurances. But then, that is the essence of faith. Rather than weaken me in pursuit of the goal, setbacks strengthen my resolve and my perseverance to the point that I know with certainty that hope is an integral part of my character.

It is your mother's church

I believe God's plan for humanity is through community. Through Abraham and the patriarchs and matriarchs and by covenant, God called a people to bear witness of God to all humanity. Today the church carries on the witnessing as a community of God.

My mother took me to Sunday School and the church community confirmed me in the faith of the church. That is the foundation that has shaped and guided me in life and that is very important in my self-understanding of who I am in society.

This is a point that has become more and more vivid to me especially when we read Verna Dozier's book, The Dream of God in our Wednesday Bible Study group at St. Mark's. We can understand Adam's fall as the fall of humanity and not individual sin. That is how we can come together as community to the flight of the afflicted and the struggling because it is humanity's affliction and suffering.

I have heard many times those who like to emphasize calls for salvation with a dismissal of "your mother's church". "It is your soul", we are told – which is true. "It's you and God, it has nothing to do with the church you grew up in, or your mother. She cannot save you".

Indeed, God has plans for every individual. Those plans however, find fulfillment in community.

I find strength, I believe we all do, in community. Bible study groups have nourished me spiritually, mentally and emotionally. In Cincinnati it was the Men's Bible study group at Christ Church Cathedral and in Washington DC, the Wednesday group. I've had shorter terms in groups at St. Paul's Cathedral in Buffalo, at Holy Trinity Lutheran Church, also in Buffalo, at Ascension and St. Agnes in Washington and Mt. Vernon United Methodist also in Washington.

Each group is different but the benefits are the same, spiritual, mental, and emotional strength. Those who come to these groups come from every walk of life and backgrounds and age groups. At St. Mark's for example, they range in age from sixties to ninety-six, mostly retirees with backgrounds in government, consultancy, academic, professional and more.

Some have been in this group for sixty years. The common experience in all these groups is the anticipation for next week. It is something to look forward to.

If it Doesn't Challenge You It Won't Change You

When I got serious enough to commit to have this book published now I also took seriously a suggestion a publishing consultant gave me. "If what is holding you back is financial", he e-mailed me, "try raising money through GoFundMe". I had heard of GoFundMe, but I had never thought of using it. Actually, fundraising in general is not my cup of tea.

But then it occurred to me too that by asking friends to support the task I am at the same time making myself accountable. Accountability exposes us to our vulnerabilities.

The second push was a quote I read somewhere that actually inspired me: "When you want something you've never had, you have to do something you've never done". It has a variant which says, "if you want something in your life you've never had, you'll have to do something you've never done". So I went to GoFundMe. It took less than thirty minutes until the fundraiser was on Facebook and less than ten minutes later two friends made donations.

This said three things to me; one, it is possible. Don't let anybody tell you, "it is not possible, you can't do it". It is strange because I intellectually knew and believed in it; yet the examples I would have been able to use for illustration would have come from other people. Here, I proved it to myself, in a small way, but that is how it becomes big.

The second lesson, we are connected, as human beings. Again, I have always believed it but we all forget sometimes; we need to be reminded from time to time. One of my friends mentioned me and my project to his friend who I had never met before. From there the connection widened through mysterious ways. I would say a byproduct of this new thing was more connections, getting to know people I never knew before. One of the new friends has a birthday two days after my birthday. I am continuing to be blown away by the possibilities. Imagine what is possible.

The third is abundance. It is a pity we live in fear of scarcity. We are ever threatened by a possibility of lacking, not having enough. Greed, hoarding, over-accumulation and the resultant huge disparity between riches and poverty are all a product of a mindset of scarcity. Truth lies in the opposite. The Universe provides abundance, there is enough love, kindness, generosity, air and water, enough land and space for everything in the Universe.

The most important resource for anyone in any situation is in a relationship. Whether on the road of recovery and wholeness, in material need, or fulfillment in life, connection is the priceless resource. Relationship is intense and demanding, giving and receiving. Because feelings and emotions are involved, it can be painful and exasperating. But it is also rewarding and fulfilling.

It is easy to give out money to a person in poverty; and if you have plenty of it, you may not even think about the act of charity, nor feel it. I am saying you can choose not to be involved emotionally. Similarly you can donate food for the hungry and those in homelessness. It is possible to serve in a soup kitchen and not get your emotions involved.

Developing and cultivating a relationship with a person in need is different. And that is what the person needs to experience transformation. It is emotional on both sides and that is why it is best avoided. Issues of trust, vulnerability, compassion and empathy make the whole dynamic too involved and uncomfortable.

Yet, again, the only way to transformation for people facing adversity, is through relationship.

Here is an example: On my first day as a volunteer for Samaritan Ministry of Greater Washington, at the entrance hallway, I ran into someone from the same parish I go to. When our eyes met he asked, "what are you doing here?" and I asked, "what are you doing here?"

It turned out he brought a young man to the ministry to see what resources were available for his need.

The young man was once employed by a maintenance company that worked for the parish. Recently the parish changed, or switched contractors, and as a result the young man lost his job. It was the right direction, to see what help was available through Samaritan Ministry, so I showed them where to go and we went our separate ways.

A couple of months later I ran into my friend again at church in between services. I asked him about his visit and any developments. He gave a deep sigh. "Oh, man", he said. "What an ordeal it has become!". What began as a quest for a job, the intake, evaluation and orientation process uncovered health issues, education, housing, transport and so on. It turned out that finding a job would be fruitless if the other issues were not addressed.

Here is another example from a parishioner who shared his experience of the difference between words or even believing and taking action. This was posted in a bulletin, again, at St.

Mark, Capitol Hill, with the title "Where I made a connection and how I carry it forward":

"There are many ways to get a glimpse of God but I know of only one that you can count on every time. That is Sunday Suppers….a program that feeds the homeless….it creates space for the servers and guests to eat together and share conversation. …Words are pretty meaningless. Especially in our current political climate.

"There is a man at Sunday Suppers who used to get very close to my face and talk emphatically about things I really did not understand. I couldn't figure out if he was giving me a spirited pep talk or a serious dressing down. It was unnerving either way. Then one Sunday I looked over and he was talking quieter and more calmly than I had ever seen before. He was talking to my son Jonathan (name changed). I could tell in the way that he whispered that he was deeply moved to be having the conversation. Everything about their interaction conveyed caring and respect. In that moment, it felt like the man loved Jonathan even more than I did, which of course feels impossible. It was my own private , beautiful miracle – a glimpse of God. And in that glimpse, my heart was broken open, filled up and put back together. I felt transformed.

"I could talk about homelessness for hours but it is nothing compared to what I experience when I actually do something about homelessness. And in the act, I receive so much more than I give"

I witnessed City Gospel Mission evolve into a relationship-based ministry with the goal of transformation. Similarly, Crossroad Health Center where I was a volunteer chaplain was founded on the principle of relationship between the medical personnel and the community they served – the latter being for the most part people of low income, in recovery, and even facing homelessness.

But, relationships develop from connections and I'll come to that in a moment.

Why is relationship important in transformation?

In my Romans class for the men in the recovery program we had the opportunity to go over Romans 12: 2 over and over again, where Paul writes: "Do not conform to the pattern of this world, but be transformed by the renewing of your mind..."

Transformation calls for a change of mindset, what Paul calls renewing of mind. Change the way you look at certain things. Change the way you see the world and that will lead to a different pattern of behavior. What Jesus told Nicodemus in John 3: 3 is the same thing. Nicodemus tried to understand it literally (a person must be born a second time) just as some Christians today misunderstand it. A person needs to be transformed from the flawed conformity. To overcome addiction, a person needs to be transformed, a change of mindset and a change of heart.

Environment has a lot to do with behavior. The people we came into contact with lived in communities beset with poverty. Some were from third generation poverty. They are used to certain lifestyles and behaviors. That is what they have known.

If there is chaos at home, parents cannot keep a steady job because of the chaos, people do not trust authority because they rely for security from one of their own, children who grow up in this environment t will behave similarly. Somebody will need to demonstrate a different lifestyle, a different possibility, for change to take place. Here we have a classic example of "show, don't tell".

Another reason why only through relationship is transformation possible can be seen in the example I gave of my friend from church and the young man who was looking for a job. Transformation leads to wholeness. Having a job – or actually, being productive in the community – is part of wholeness. There are other components too that are needed to complete the picture. Through relationship one is enabled to discover and address those essential components.

In every shelter and every program, people are eager to find a job. Even in residential recovery programs one of the main complaints is, "why can't we go to work?" The most common and frequent prayer request in homeless shelters is for work. Similarly, the most common testimony is how God has intervened to provide one with a job. Unfortunately finding a job often leads to falling back to old destructive ways, or the job does not last for lack of preparation and any chaos not taken care of .

In her book, The Dream of God, Verna Dozier decries the church's over-emphasis on spirituality at the expense of social justice. This is in reference to some churches for sure, but it represents a very large segment of the church.

In a shelter in Washington DC, for example, there is an evening chapel service every day for the residents of the shelter. Some residents are in a recovery program but the majority are overnight guests. After dinner, all assemble in the chapel for a mandatory reading of rules of the shelter. One of the rules reads: "Because we are a Christian Ministry there is no smoking, drinking alcoholic beverages or the use of illegal drugs permitted in the building".

It sounds unnecessary to predicate the rule in a Christian premise because it gives credence to the perception that Christianity is a set of rules and regulations. Structure is very important, especially when you have a group of people in homelessness.

Homelessness and poverty are characterized with chaos and sporadic behavior. One of the major adjustments required to move from homelessness to a home or from poverty to abundance or sufficiency is structure, including the discipline of planning.

Where you have a group of people, or a community, some regulations are needed. Christianity embodies some principles that would be sufficient for any community. For example a Christian would refrain from smoking in a building where others reside. Many communities already have statutes regulating designated areas for smoking and drinking alcohol.

This is not to suggest that Christians are the best disciplined. Christians, like anybody else abuse freedoms. The point is that these rules are common sense regulations for everybody, Christian, agnostic, atheist, Muslim or Budhist.

As Verna points out, saving individual souls for eternal life ought not be the only goal. Often the claim made is that once a person is "saved", or connected with Jesus, the afflictions they are dealing with disappear.

At City Gospel Mission, dinner is served everyday (and breakfast too) for shelter residents and the public. For many years, a chapel service – mostly preaching – preceded dinner. In practice what happened was that to be served dinner one attended chapel service – after all, they could accommodate only so many before the doors closed.

As you can imagine, what happened during the preaching was chaos. Those in attendance showed up to eat. They hardly paid attention to the preaching and most of the time there were all kinds of disruption going on: sleeping, loud conversations, arguing and even fighting. The volunteer churches saw their mission to be saving souls for Christ.

The Mission came to the realization that it had its priorities wrong and decided to adopt a relational approach. Feed the hungry first, engage and connect with them, invite them to a chapel service after dinner and continue the engagement and connection. But the majority of the volunteer churches accused the Mission of abandoning the Christian call, packed up and gave up their ministry.

It is a lot easier to preach from a pulpit to individuals you don't know except that they are either hungry, poor, or homeless, or all three.   Connecting with them means getting to know them beyond their hunger, poverty and homelessness. That is a lot more demanding, but it is the only way to transformation and wholeness.

Thus, ministry to the needy often takes one or the other of two directions. On the one hand you have what can be referred to as the "traditional Protestant and Catholic" approach, exemplified by the testimony in St. Mark's bulletin quoted above. It can also be summarized in these words of St. Teresa of Avila: "Christ has no body now, but yours. No hands, no feet on earth, but yours. Yours are the eyes through which Christ looks compassion into the world. Yours are the feet with which Christ walks to do good. Yours are the hands with which Christ blesses the world".

I see in this model Matthew 25: 31-46, "   and the King will answer them, "Truly, I say to you, as you did it to one of the least of these my brothers you did it to me….as you did not do it to one of the least of these my brothers, you did not do it to me".

In the second approach, typically by Evangelical churches and groups, services provided are secondary to a more urgent mission of conversion. The claim is that the needy are in the situation they are in because they lack Christ in their lives and, should they accept Jesus their adversities will be gone.

With this mindset, accepting Jesus is as simple as making a public verbal confession and believing in one's heart since, literally, scripture says, "for it is with your heart that you believe and are justified, and it is with your mouth that you profess your faith and are saved" Romans 10:10).Believe in your heart, and confess with your mouth and that is it. You are saved.

Unfortunately, believing is a product of rationale. I believe because I have reason to believe. There is a foundation upon which belief stands. But even more problematic is the obvious contradiction that those instant converts experience between their promised new life and real life. Some individuals find it necessary to "accept" the altar call multiple times. They must not "believe" that anything has changed even as they are reassured that they have been saved instantly.

Ron had been in a program at Buffalo City Mission for five years. He went through the acceptance calls many times, according to his confession. One of his major frustrations was anger. He talked about it every time there was occasion to seek advice from those around him.

Everybody felt his anger, especially at mealtime. He was charged with security detail, standing at the door to ensure orderly conduct into the dining room and during meals. There was always cause for him to want to choke a guest or to throw somebody out. It could be a resident who forgot his badge, a guest with a hat on or someone who spoke in the middle of the benediction for meals or a guest who lingered on for too long after Ron declared mealtime over.

To be sure, some of these were clearly infringements of shelter regulations, but to him, everything was a major disregard that he could not deal with. Occasionally the chaplain removed him from certain responsibilities due to his uncontrollable anger ,but every interaction he had with anyone was a contest.

He wanted to be able to control his anger, he confessed, and he asked for suggestions as to how to win the battle. He found no solution, he agonized, and deep in his heart his outbursts of rage made him doubt the salvation he was promised.

The bottom line is that believing is meaningless if that belief does not manifest in some change in attitude, behavior and character. Addiction recovery programs emphasize an attitude of humility and meekness. So a person who testifies to have been delivered by Jesus – when he professed belief (often juxtaposed, erroneously, with faith) – will manifest humility, not arrogance, honesty not lies, kindness rather than rage. And when these qualities are not forthcoming, what people see is a display of piety or empty words not supported by appropriate behavior.

Most shelters promote graduates of their various programs into staff positions, which is commendable. Unfortunately, pride remains the biggest temptation for the new recruits.

In the Hebrew bible, the Israelites' commandments regarding the less fortunate, the needy and the afflicted end with the reminder, "because/remember, you were slaves in Egypt". The Israelites were prone to forget this, and staff recruits who were once afflicted tend to succumb to exaltation instead of humility. There may even be tendencies towards condescending or outright despising. In these circumstances, testimonies of salvation or deliverance are seen as acting and make-belief.

At worst, what really comes out is piety – but this will be one of the topics I address fully in a future publication.

Compassion and Humility

We come across ministries bearing the title Matthew 25 in reference to Matthew 25: 31-46, the separation and judgment of sheep and goats. Almost anyone involved in social justice ministry has, in various degrees, this passage in mind. Some politicians too have it in their conscience, as exemplified by Ohio Governor John Kasich's comment in the Columbus Dispatch of June 19, 2013: "Now, when you die and get to the meeting with St. Peter, he's probably not going to ask you much about what you did about keeping government small. But he is going to ask you what you did for the poor. You better have a good answer".

But then, when I look at Jesus' story, especially in the context of today culture with all the revelations of injustice and above by those with power, I wonder why Jesus is talking of separating goats and sheep and not wolves. More significantly though, is the shock by both groups. Those commended for doing good are stunned. "When did we do all this? We were not aware we served you".

This is a lesson in compassion and humility. Serving the needy is an act of compassion which becomes part of someone's life. Eventually we are no longer thinking about it; it is part of who we are. Or, at least that is how it should be.

Often times though, that is not how it is. It is tempting to want to see outcomes, mostly the outcomes we want. I have seen in some social service endeavors, patrons whose sole aim is winning souls for Jesus. Yet, true blessing from this ministry is, as already pointed out, the opportunity for an encounter with God.

Many volunteers I have worked with testify that the experience of serving leaves them feeling fulfilled than what they think they gave. I know from personal experience that when it is time to go home after a volunteer engagement, I experience gratefulness and satisfaction. Even on those days when I have not felt particularly driven to go and may even be in doubt whether to go or not, I end up thanking God for that push that made me go because I end up uplifted.

My volunteer work at Charlie's Place, a social ministry of St. Margaret's Episcopal Church began with serving breakfast at 6:30 in the morning. This experience reminded me of those volunteers I worked with at City Gospel Mission who had to get started at 4 in the morning to get breakfast ready at 7. At Charlie's Place volunteers arrived at 6:30. I set out around 5:30 on a bike ride and always looked forward to the experience.

After a short period it struck me that the guests there, so early in the morning, were unusually calm and orderly in comparison to other venues I am familiar with. The guests sat down at tables, came up to the serving table for coffee and pastries before breakfast was served; there was no shoveling, arguing, cussing or foul language.

I even made a remark to the program manager about the exemplary behavior, and he said to me, "we keep it that way". Yet, no orders or commands were made by the staff or volunteers. The only time the staff on duty addressed the guests together was when calling attention for benediction and to announce a summary of activities available after breakfast and in coming days.

The Volunteer Information Sheet states the following: "Taking the time to talk to our clients is an important part of your volunteer experience, and very much appreciated by our clients". Indeed, in its mission, Charlie's Place stresses that nurturing the spirit is through respect, civility, care and fellowship, offering our clients a safe, quiet and companionable space". With this mindset, no rules, orders, directives are necessary.

There are other ministries in Washington DC where guests get, in addition to breakfast and lunch, showers, their laundry done, bus tokens, mail delivery, computer lab and referrals for legal assistance. Several centers actually provide these services if not every day of the week, at least regularly throughout the week. In some of these centers, clients must go through intake with a counselor.

From time to time, one counselor in one of these centers finds it necessary to chastise the clients, publicly, with the intention to admonish (to use St. Paul's term) or to encourage action. He reminds them that lunch is available only to those who, after breakfast, participate in the activities offered between breakfast and lunch. One of the rules of the center is "no sleeping". Visitors must participate in some of the activities offered. There is no lunch for people coming in just to eat and anyone in the building may not be there simply to rest or catch up with sleep.

Indeed there are centers where guests watch T.V all day. In between they nap and eat, step outside to smoke cigarettes or weed, or even something stronger. You can perhaps understand the counselor's point. And, as is the case everywhere, ninety five percent of the guests are the same people you see everday.

So he complains of people who do not show progress. Some have been coming for services for years and in his view, it is because of lack of commitment to the values exposed to them every day, and there is truth in it.

One day he decided to be very candid with the clients. "Do you think I want to come here to this ministry every day? Why do you think I am coming here every day? Let me tell you: what I would want to do is sell drugs. But I know the damage that business did to me and my family. I come here every day to keep me away from the lifestyle that stole decades from my life. God, by grace, saved me from that life and I made a commitment to myself. And every day I am coming here because I made a commitment".

He paused as the chapel where the clients assemble went into total silence. Some were probably still selling drugs, either he knew it or he suspected that much. Then he continued,

"Ihear some of you saying, 'man, they feed us good!' Just think of what you are saying, "they feed us good!" You are human beings; you don't feed human beings. You feed animals and pets. And you go around boasting of being fed. That is why I am frustrated because some of you have lost what it means to be human. You have been here too long".

Preachers too, especially those who have personal background of addiction, are similarly prone to use their personal experience to chastise in the form of testimony. There is a note of urgency because they are afraid of slipping back to the destructive lifestyle.

You can hear the pleading: "Listen man! I have altogether fifteen children and grandchildren. I'm sixty-two and spent fourteen years in prison. Man, I am ashamed of the legacy I tried to leave to them. I used the basement in my house to teach them all kinds of crazy stuff, but I thought it was cool. I would teach them how to shoot a gun, how to hustle and intimidate customers. I wanted them to imitate me, but I did not know anything else. I was a slave, now I am free, I have choices. Man, don't let anybody tell you, "they did this or that to me". No, you have a choice, nobody makes you do anything".

People who have been there know the pain and damage they inflicted on themselves and on others, especially their children. Now they are afraid of thinking of the possibility of slipping back. Dealing with that fear can sometimes come out as biting chastisement.

The Law Condemns The Best of Us; But Grace Saves The Worst of Us

There is a lot of meaning in these words of the Singaporean charismatic pastor, Joseph Prince. Ministry to the needy or the afflicted can sometimes feel like attempting to balance law and grace and for the naive it may sound like a literal meaning og Galatians 5: 23, "But the fruit of the Spirit is love, joy, peace, patience, kindness, goodness, faithfulness, gentleness, and self-control. Against these things there is no law".

Some of the briefing we gave to volunteers who came in for Outreach Ministry (the Outlet) at City Gospel Mission, or in any capacity, was, essentially, not to be naive when engaging with clients. The following is verbatim from a Volunteers Guidelines Information and you will find similar guidelines in any ministry:

"We want volunteers to get to know the people we help; however, be careful about being naive. Many times, people who are disadvantaged have learned to survive by becoming adept at using others. Volunteers should remain on a first name basis. Do not give your last name, address, telephone number, e-mail or any personal information to any guests or program participants.

Also: Do not give or loan money to anyone; Do not give rides or take anyone to your home without approval; Do not be alone with someone of the opposite sex."

Even though you are trying to connect, you also need to be careful, in other words. It is not easy at all. At City Gospel Mission we had staff meeting first thing on Monday morning and a major part of the meeting was my weekend report since I was the only one working weekends while everybody was at work during the week. A lot of times during those meetings my superior looked at me with sympathy and this question: "Is it difficult to balance between law and grace?".

Whether we like it or not, in this ministry that balance is always a difficult path. The advice given to volunteers may appear restrictive but it is also necessary to know where boundaries are.

Manipulative and Guilt Trips

Many years ago and straight from college I lived in a hostel owned by Catholic nuns. After a few months, and due to my own fault I was behind on my rent so I asked the nuns for an extension of time which they kindly granted. Still I was unable to be current on my rent.

They summoned me to the office and gave me a notice: get the rent up to date or move out. That actually shocked me because it went beyond a nun's sense of kindness, so I employed guilt trips though at that time I did not see it in that light. "This is un-Christian", I said. But she stood her ground; she was not accepting my accusation. She reminded me that I too had responsibilities to abide to.

Fast-forward and years later I would occasionally be on the receiving end. Some guests coming in to the Outlet Outreach Ministry for example would find something to resist a simple requirements to sign in. The need to sign in was simply part of our overall goal to provide a safe environment. But there were those who demanded that a Christian place be free of any requirements simply because "you are Christians and we are guests".

Manipulation is a weapon of the disadvantaged as also is a sense of entitlement. I had to learn from experience that kindness is not weakness. We get to learn too, that our guests have not benefitted from structured living. So they come into a facility that is alien to their experience. Many are suspicious of authority figures because a good part of their interaction with authority was when they were in trouble.

Volunteer work reminds me of some speeches that government officials in Tanzania made when they were invited to ordination ceremonies. They always expressed the optimism that the church helps government in their connections with the people because "when the police get involved it is a show of authority".

At the end of the day, we benefit when we realize that the desire and temptation to control – situations and others – is so volatile that the negative energy fuels conflict. It was obvious to many in the example of Ron, for example, that his anger was fueled by his mindset of being in control. That works both ways, for staff and guests alike.

There is Power in Being Vulnerable

A young priest in a progressive parish recently captured my imagination in a sermon on Luke 4: 16-22. In this gospel Jesus returns to Nazareth after his temptation in the desert. He goes into the synagogue on Sabbath, reads from Isaiah 61 and proclaims it to be his mission. We read that the people are amazed at his gracefulness and that is it. But if we read a few verses ahead, the same people seek to hurl him down a cliff.

There is no doubt that this story is edited for the church and will find open minds in a progressive congregation where it is easy for us to identify ourselves as Jesus' followers who are carrying forward his mission. "…proclaim good news to the poor…proclaim freedom for the prisoners and recovery of sight for the blind, to set the oppressed free and to proclaim the year of the Lord's favor".

For a progressive congregation, social justice may sound as the ultimate call. With it lies the danger of seeing the poor, the homeless, the oppressed, the prisoner only in those that we serve. Suppose we see ourselves as the poor, the prisoner and the oppressed.

The priest suggested that perhaps Jesus' mission is found in Matthew 1: 23 which is borrowed from Isaiah 7:14, "you shall call him Immanuel (God with us)". This way we see Jesus' mission as "God with us", God in our midst, in our sorrows and anxieties, in our struggles and aspirations.

This opens us up and exposes us as to who we truly are. We live in a society of conformity and searching to belong. I have heard this charge many times in ministry to the marginalized. There is a difference between the façade we put forward and our true selves. And of course, the healthy life is being who we really are.

The young priest's sermon reminded me of my vulnerabilities. Here is one example.

Because of the awkward situation with my visa status, City Gospel Mission could not put me in their payroll. I lived in a Mission apartment, fully furnished, utilities paid for, got free meals and even clothing. I did not have any of the normal expenses that a renter incurs. In return my ministry was of volunteer status.

One day, a photo-journalist was asking for stories about homelessness for an online story. My gut feeling was that my situation was unique, given my background, and also there were illustrations in my experience of the complexity of immigration issues and the resultant misunderstandings.

I knew too, that technically, anyone living in housing they don't pay rent or related expenses, if they are living with relatives or friends, as long as they retain no possession or control of the premises, that is homelessness. I volunteered to share my story for advocacy purposes.

If City Gospel Mission had not provided accommodations for me I would have been on the streets or in my car or in a shelter. As a matter of fact, at that particular moment I did not know of a friend I could have lodged in with. Moreover, I knew there are many others like me who have been driven to the precipice because of political calculation. Able-bodied and highly qualified individuals with tremendous potential to contribute to the well-being of society but relegated to the margins of society purely for political gains.

Let's face it: Everybody makes mistakes. It is natural. And of course mistakes can be costly. But they are not irreparable. I have always looked at it this way. A person may, for example, fail to pay taxes, even if by negligence. Still there is remedy for that, which is, pay what you owe, plus penalties and interest, then pick up from there and continue with life. Immigration, on the other hand, is like an irredeemable curse.

Now, my decision to share my story was a gut decision, but later my head got involved and I called the journalist and informed her that I changed my mind. I did not want the story published, especially after I realized there was a lot of stereotypes projected by the photo-journalist. She said she would let the editors know of the change of mind and the story would not be published.

Three or four months later, the story appeared online and I was furious. I called everybody including the managing editor, fumed, protested and just wanted the story deleted but they would not. So, I had to live with it, with bitterness and misgiving. I even published my own thoughts about their lack of integrity, betrayal and unfaithfulness.

I felt vulnerable, which I was not ready to embrace at that time. I was still in appearance management state. Indeed, we should embrace being vulnerable but it can also be painful in the beginning. However, it is worth far more than all the short term gains.

Several months later and I was in Washington and I was beginning to connect with one parish and the pastor had all these ideas about possible areas of ministry I could be of help. We even made an appointment for consultation with an immigration agency – even though I had been informed of the predicament of my situation several times in the past. The pastor was optimistic because he had had some successes with some immigrants in the past and my philosophy is always to be open for any possibilities.

On the way the pastor informed me that one of the parishioners was going to help me with housing for two months. It felt like there could be good miracles out of our immigration consultation. But as I expected, I got the same information I had been given so many times in the past.

The young lawyer even diverted from giving legal advice to a lengthy exploration of her memory of honeymooning in Tanzania, even as she could not remember the town she was in. There was no Arusha connection. And in the meantime, the pastor must have been busy online because suddenly he asked, with clear shock in his eyes, "and, were you homeless?".

My vulnerability! I felt numb. This was a congregation that has extensive involvement in social ministry and issues of social justice. I tried to give him the background and meaning of the online story but he suddenly announced, "the lady who was going to help with an apartment said she will not be able to help if there is a problem with immigration because she works for the Justice Department" I could not help laughing aloud as I reflected on the irony of helping if no help is needed, but then there was the shame to deal with.

I shared the young priest's sermon with our bible study group because it resonated with a topic we were discussing that week. We were reading Verna Dozier's book, The Dream of God. Towards the end of chapter two, Verna comments about Jesus beginning his ministry. She writes: "Jesus had a significant religious experience in which he understood who he was and what he was called to be. That baptism was followed by a lengthy period in which he wrestled through how best to present to his people God's ancient call to them to be something new in the world. By concern to the marginalized?

"That had always been a significant part of Israel's covenant with God, but it could be distorted into a means of getting credit with God instead of an expression of the very nature of God. By taking over the kingdoms of the world and compelling them to serve God? But God's ends can only be achieved by

God's means. By a spectacular demonstration of the good effects of allegiance to God? But to demand proof from God denies God's omnipotence"

So we have three temptations; turn stones into bread, have dominion over kingdoms, perform miraculous acts.

For those absorbed in social justice, like progressive congregations, feeding the hungry and advocating for the incarcerated for example, can translate into self-righteousness or even deserving acts that make God indebted. Similarly, relationships with civil authorities and government may not differ from gaining dominions and kingdoms. And indeed, there are many who would like to boast of miraculous achievements in ministry, similar to Jesus throwing himself from the temple to demonstrate his authority.

Perhaps our call then is to see ourselves as the poor and the prisoners. That exposes our vulnerabilities.

What is Important? The 5000 Club

I was part of the ministry of the 5000 Club at Christ Church
Cathedral. It was a street ministry and as the name implies was
founded on Jesus' miraculous feeding of a multitude of 5000
with five loaves of bread and two fish, according to Matthew
14:13-21; Mark 6:30-44; and Luke 9:10-17.

The vision of the founders of the service was to provide
quality, hot and homemade dinner to anyone on the street. The
idea was to create an experience for the guests, of a catered
meal, served at white cloth tables, complete with china
silverware for a memorable evening. Along with dinner,
caseworkers would also be on hand for social services as well
as medical check-ups and necessary assistance.

This was a once a week event and the attendance was
always above capacity and much anticipated. We began with

evening prayer, for any who wanted to attend and those who attended got preference for the dinner after the service. The idea was that gradually the evening service would be integrated into the weekly liturgy and those who attended become an integral part of the cathedral community.

Except for the evening prayer which took place in the chapel, all the services, and dinner, were provided in the undercroft. The same space was also reserved, once a quarter, for an interfaith group that used undercroft to host homeless families for a week.

On the one quarterly one evening when the undercroft was used for families, the 5000 Club dinner was served in Styrofoam containers and guests could eat in the hallway where temporary seating was provided or carry-out.

Then came the burn-out. Stretched out kitchen volunteers needed a break. At a volunteers meeting they suggested that when guest families were hosted in the undercroft, we should skip the 5000 Club services altogether. This would give the kitchen staff some much needed rest.

Not everyone was in favor, especially due to the popularity of the ministry among the guests. But one of the founders of the club made the convincing argument. He reminded everyone the principal features of the dinners: seating guests at white table cloth tables, hot meal and china silverware. Without that, the service would have failed in its objectives.

And this is the point of this story. First of all, the decision was subsequently rebuked by the dean of the cathedral. Here we have an example of different perspectives by two different social classes. The volunteers represent the upper, or rich, class. How food is presented is important for this group. They are satisfied with an almost empty plate with decorative arrangements and white cloth and silverware.

For the poor, the hungry and the needy, presentation is meaningless. Quantity, no matter how it is served, is what matters. On Styrofoam containers, standing up or carry out is okay as long as there is food. How do you tell the hungry they are not eating today because of silverware?

Perfectionism

But I always feel that whatever I do, I could do better. suppose it is perfectionism – *(Rowan Atkinson)*

Society emphasizes perfection, achievement, success. We are scared to be anything less. We don't want to admit that we are struggling because we'll look imperfect. Society conditions us for perfection, not sufficiency.

I am a perfectionist. Not that I chose to be one, because one does not choose. I sometimes console myself that I am not the freak perfectionist; the one who arranges things by color and gets things done one way and one way only. That is no consolation, however because perfectionism is perfectionism and there is nothing positive in it.

I grew up being praised, by my mother and my teachers. "Straight to Makerere", was Teacher August's congratulatory declaration whenever I rescued the class with the correct answer. And from that early on, if I got it wrong, and, God forbid, a classmate got the correct answer, I sobbed publicly.

In Middle School, the teachers used me to shame those in higher grade. When they could not get the correct answer, I would be summoned to appear in front of the class and give the answer. I can still picture myself in Standard V standing in front of staring Standard VII kids who did not know the difference between a lamp and a lump.

I know my mother and my teachers had the best intentions for me. The outcome has been crippling. In college and graduate school, at the end of the semester I always asked for an extension to submit my paper. I needed to work on it over and over because I was never satisfied that it was good enough.

Psychologists and psychiatrists agree that there is distinction between adaptive or healthy perfectionism and maladaptive or unhealthy perfectionism in that"...adaptive/healthy perfectionism tends to be associated with good psychological well-being and high achievement...maladaptive/unhealthy perfectionism has been associated with distress, low self-esteem and symptoms of mental illness". So here also we see society's perspective: achievement. By necessity, achievement is competitive and it is inadequate.

Furthermore, as I try to be transparent, I have to acknowledge that at times I am judgmental as I tend to not recognize others' achievements. Judgment comes from comparison. It is all in the exercise of perfection. The perfectionist strives to be better than the other person and unfortunately there is no end to the pursuit.

But this is also harmful to others. It is important that we appreciate other people's efforts and contribution. For the perfectionist everybody else is deficient. The effort is not enough, what they have is not good enough.

This was one of the challenges I had to face as I was in a position of helping people struggling with addictions. To me perfectionism feels like a compulsive disorder in that it has no optimum capacity. It demands more and more. But the main struggle was to be able to see and appreciate adequacy in others and in myself.

That is a problem that projects on oneself also. What a perfectionist demands of others he/she demands on self too. Inadequacy, not good enough, past mistakes and the day's struggles as a result of the past can weigh heavily on anyone seeking to put addiction behind.

Two passages in Paul's epistle to the Romans gave us the assurance of healing. Romans 5: 1 and 8: 1 both have the adverb "therefore" which in this case is both consequential as well as a bridge from the past to the present. In view of what has happened between us and God (through Jesus Christ), now we are reconciled with God and with ourselves. Now – at the present time – we carry no condemnation in our hearts and minds (at least we shouldn't).

We can now move on without any feelings of inadequacy, fears of past failures, and anxieties of imperfection. That was the process of healing for those recovering from addiction and also the perfectionists like me. I can live a free life without the burdens of perfectionism. This I learned in my connections with the disadvantaged, the sick and without adequate health insurance, the immigrant living in fear and many of those living on the precipice.

When I was a seminary professor I earned the accolade of a brilliant teacher. There was always anticipation for my sermons in the chapel. What nobody knew was the time it took me to prepare for my lectures and sermons. In fact those who knew of my extensive preparations, mostly fellow professors, saw that as a positive endeavor.

I too thought it an accomplishment to be thoroughly prepared. But beyond being prepared was this feeling that I had not prepared enough. After all those hours it was still not enough. I was unable to accept that we will never attain perfection.

No One is Alone

Dr. John Perkins is a well-known Christian minister and community developer, among many other accomplishments. Initially driven by evangelism, he later came to the realization that the Christian Good News is concerned with both spiritual and physical human needs. In his 1976 book, "A Quiet Revolution": The Christian Response to human need, a strategy for today, he expounds on what he calls the 3 R's of Christian ministry as Relocation, Redistribution, and Reconciliation.

In response to the 3 R's, four members of a bible study group in Cincinnati (Sycamore Street Fellowship), Sally Stewart, Janet Germann, Julie and Chuck Schubert founded Crossroad Health Center in Cincinnati's Over the Rhine. Connecting with the people they wanted to serve involved forming community with them, and moving into their neighborhood. As a volunteer chaplain at the center, I needed a change of mindset and an open mind.

Let me explain what I mean by that, then cite an example. It is often difficult for middle class suburban volunteers to cross over the divide between the unspoken "us" and "them". There is some uneasiness when one group is perceived to be on the giving end and the other group on the receiving side.

All kinds of emotions can come into play, often inadvertently: Shame, blaming, patronizing, condescending, not belonging or unworthy and so on.

It is always uplifting, and counted as a blessing, when a volunteer connects with a needy client and the two can relate to each other as equals, free from emotional burdens. Indeed, volunteering is meaningful and fulfilling when connection is achieved. It was common practice at the center that the medical personnel prayed with their patients, whenever there was opportunity.

Because of the doctors' and nurses' commitment to the spiritual well-being of their patients, I saw my service there as a chaplain as an opportunity to allow them more time for the physical diagnosis while I tended to the spiritual. Still, the connection was so strong that many patients expected to have some time of prayer with their doctor.

I have since seen more of this dynamic in Washington where medical personnel engage in outreach to the needy and vulnerable and develop connections. My PCP introduced me to a volunteer opportunity where the bond between the providers and recipients of services have cultivated a mutual give-and-take relationship and trust.

Anyway, at Crossroad the majority of the patients were African American and Latino/a. I discovered that we had a lot in common, for example health issues, like diabetes.

One day a nurse sent a patient to me because he was distraught after he learned that he was diabetic. He was not even sure if he needed me talking to him, it seemed like he was only being polite after the nurse persuaded him to talk to the chaplain.

"It is not a death sentence my brother", I patted his shoulder. "I have been diabetic for twenty years and I am still here". He turned abruptly to look at me in the eye. "Get out of here", he said. I noticed his face was beginning to relax. "You are not serious, are you?" I told him I was dead serious, that I have been on insulin for quite some time and that life goes on, that the only time I think of my diabetes is when I am injecting insulin.

The good thing about us diabetics, I told him, is that we learn to own it and speak of "my diabetes". By now he had lightened up and was listening with what appeared to me to be fascination. I went on to tell him how I felt devastated that day, more than twenty years ago, when I was told I was diabetic.

There was a rash on a most unlikely part of my body that just seemed to go nowhere. It looked like a scratch on the skin. It did not heal, it did not hurt, it did not grow, it just stayed there. That was why I decided to go to the Emergency Room at Christ Hospital because it should have healed for its tiny size or it should have gotten worse. But it did not. For days, it just stayed there.

To my surprise, the ER doctor could not give me a ready prognosis either. He ordered some blood tests and I sat there behind the white curtains and waited for what felt like eternity. Soon I began to dose off, then I woke up to the doctor abruptly parting the curtains. "You are diabetic", he announced. Your blood sugar level is three times the normal level".

I heard the words but they did not register any meaning at that point. "I want you to take this seriously", he was saying. "I'll give you some medication, but I want you to make an appointment with your physician and a nutritionist..." My mind was blank.

The only thing I knew about diabetes was that a disproportionate number of pastors at home in Tanzania had a sugar problem. It was only later that I was able to conclude that perhaps it wasn't a pastors' disease but they had better access to medical attention and early detection. When the ER doctor asked me about family history of diabetes, I did not have one because no one in my immediate family had ever been diagnosed with the condition. It may have existed undetected.

Then it was my turn to ask him a question. "What causes diabetes?" It was not something I had ever thought about. His response? "If you can find out what causes diabetes, you'll be awarded a Nobel Prize".

At this point my new friend at the clinic and I had made a connection. "It's something we'll have to live with", I reassured him. "We probably won't be cured, but we'll manage and control it. We won't let it control us". We reflected together on St. Paul's words in 2 Corinthians 12 concerning the thorn in the flesh. No doubt, something in Paul's life, a weakness or infirmity, something he does not specify bothered him. He wanted it gone, like diabetes. But the Lord said to him, "my grace is sufficient".

There is plenty of grace in spite of "our diabetes". I have never been sad on account of my diabetes. On the contrary I have been able to live without any shadow of diabetes hanging over me. I have been able to count on all the blessings of life and, with gratitude, have been able to live with joy.

I am glad that my friend was able to overcome the fear of diabetes. I shared with him my own apprehension for the needle when it was time to begin insulin. Eventually it is not even an inconvenience. He too was ready and from then on, whenever he came to the clinic we talked about diet and exercise. We both enjoyed both. In fact his initial shock was because he went to the gym every day before his diagnosis, but now the gym became even more a source of enjoyment and fun.

It Doesn't Have to be That Way

It is said that life is only as good as your mindset. Mindset, or perspective, is huge for every individual and every society or community.

Over the years we have talked, strategized, advocated and prayed to end poverty. Often we have come up with what we thought to be achievable goals, like, "to end poverty in and homelessness in 30 years". But sadly, year after year, it looks like a losing battle. The major obstacle is the system and the accompanying mindset.

I was excited when the community builder, Peter Block and the Hebrew Bible theologian Walter Brueggermann led a grassroots effort to rethink our current narrative and be bold enough to re-imagine an alternative way of life.

Some people have recognized that our economic narrative is exploitative, mean, oppressive and despite the desire and pledges "to end poverty and homelessness", the poor and homeless are casualties of our current economic system.

Many people feel the pain. Many know that something needs to change, that the current situation cannot be sustained. This realization led to the inception of the Economics of Compassion Initiative of Greater Cincinnati, on the premise that every community can imagine and create a caring, compassionate and inclusive system that works for everyone. It is possible and necessary to imagine an alternative.

In a discussion of Bernard Brandon Scott's book, Re-Imagine the World, at St. Mark's I attempted to relate Jesus' parables of the Kingdom of God with many of our imaginings in the Economics of Compassion Initiative.

This is how Scott's book is summarized, in part, on the back cover: "In his parables Jesus re-imagines the world. The re-imagined world, called the Kingdom of God, presents his followers with a new option for living, one that contrasts with the default world of the everyday. The new world is both terrifying and liberating..."

The resonance of the Gospel with economics of compassion makes my experience in the Economics of Compassion Initiative ever present in my daily life.

For the Fifteenth Sunday after Pentecost Gospel Reading from Matthew 20: 1-16, my contribution in the Men's Bible Study group at Christ Church Cathedral was a reflection on Gift Economy and Economy of Generosity in the Kingdom of God which I posted in my blog.

The parable of the workers in the vineyard illustrates that the model economy in the Kingdom of God is generosity, or gift economy, not our "free market" economy. It is interesting that the NIV gives a title for the parable, Workers in the Vineyard, suggesting an interpretation with emphasis on the workers. Yet the point Jesus is making in this parable is found in the double question, "Am I not allowed to do what I choose with what belongs to me? Or are you envious because I am generous?"

In our market economy the answer to both questions is affirmative. The affirmation in the first question though is problematic. Today we have many examples of celebrities who believed they earned the right to do whatever they chose because they have worked hard only to discover they have been misguided.

The second part of the question brings to mind the older brother in the parable of the lost son, or prodigal in Luke 15: 11-32 who complains, "all these years I have toiled for you and you have never given me even a young goat to celebrate".

In both parables, the disgruntled are raising the issue of merit and deserving. They deserve, the favored are undeserving. Both parables give a good picture of the early workers' and the older brother's self-interest on the one hand and the landowner's and the father's generosity on the other.

The landowner is God, as the father is. The vineyard is the Kingdom of God. In God's Kingdom, God provides for the needs of all, not on the basis of merit or deserving, but solely by grace. Nobody earns or has claim on God's provision, it is only by grace, and God's grace is plentiful and it covers all.

We can see in this parable that God is interested in the welfare of all. A worker needs a day's wages for personal and family support; that is the need God meets out of God's generosity not on anyone's merit. In a gift economy as this parable illustrates, the motivating factor is generosity not self-interest, or profit as a human landowner would seek. The mindset is that of giving and receiving, as opposed to selling and buying. It's a mindset of a world of abundance and sufficiency instead of scarcity and competition.

Competition breeds jealousy and envy, as the parable illustrates. Furthermore, competition fuels anxiety, the natural consequence of the market economy. On the other hand, the hallmark of the Kingdom of God, the mindset Jesus is urging his followers to imagine, is a gift economy built on generosity and cooperation.

The theological foundation of the Economics of Compassion Initiative was laid out by Dr. Walter Brueggermann in session after session at different venues. Incidentally there are similar initiatives in different communities around the world, all of which espouse creative ways of dissociating from the default economic narrative. Often in his lectures, Dr. Brueggermann drew on the similarities between Pharaoh's economy in Genesis 41 and our market economy.

As he puts it, Pharaoh had nightmares which can be compared to the anxiety we experience today. Pharaoh's nightmares prompted him to expand production and to build storehouses. Our economy is driven by production and consumption – ever expanding productivity, competition, and profit maximization. This does not only fuel anxiety and nightmares but it also results in waste and exploitation.

On the Way to Kibbutz Regavim

Having expressed the desire to live in a kibbutz for three months as a volunteer, my friends at the Swedish Theological Institute set about looking for one that would be of mutual benefit to me and to the kibbutz. They did not have many choices because I was already in my early thirties. Volunteers were mostly high school and college kids. So they found Kibbutz Regavim

Located near Caesarea, Regavim could be reached only by train, if using public transport, and the train service was once a day. My plan was to travel by bus from Haifa after a weekend tour with my Ugandan priest friend, to Netanya and Hadera then catch the train to Binyamina.

I arrived in Netanya a little before six. The sun was orange over the Mediterranean Sea to the west where it appeared to be sinking into the water. It was calm and comfortable late Spring the air seeming to soothe the skin.

It was the first time I was in Netanya – I might have passed through between Jerusalem and Haifa, but unlikely. I roamed along the beach for a while, then up and down Sderot Weizmann, Yehuda Hanasi and Perach Tikva hoping to find a cheap motel for the night then take the bus to Hadera and the train to Binyamina. Then I realized I was in a wrong neighborhood.

I decided to seek help. It was Sunday, the first day of the week, businesses were still open and I spotted a real estate office. I walked into this rather small office with a couple of desks. There was only one person behind one of the desks, so I asked him if he knew of any cheap motel in the area.

He looked up at me and said, "There are many hotels on the beach". I almost chuckled at the suggestion but I thought he misunderstood my query. "I know, but I cannot afford a hotel room on the beach

I explained to him that I needed to catch a train on Monday from Hadera to Binyamina and to Kibbutz Regavim. He looked at me quizzically then repeated what he told me. "There are many hotels along the beach".

I started to turn around to leave his office when he asked, "Do you really need help?" I told him I did. He told me to come back after an hour and he would see how he could help. I went back an hour later and found him closing his office.

He told me, his name is Avner, that he and his mother and a younger brother lived in a *Moshav* nearby and if I really needed help I was invited to stay the night with them. A stranger, from nowhere! Was this chance, or coincidence? You decide.

So he took me to their home. His mother was recently widowed, they had just finished the *shiva,* the seven day mourning period after burial. His younger brother, Moshe, was seriously wounded in combat, he still had a bullet lodged in his head. He was active, even drove a special car, but he was disabled.

 This family took me to their home, a complete stranger, from a strange land, different nationality, religion, culture and all that. But they welcomed me. When I left the following morning to catch the bus to Hadera, ima, mother to Avner and Moshe, and now mine too, said to me, "remember you have a home in Israel; this is your home".

And so, I believe that, as human beings, we are connected and it is the essence of humanity. Spirituality, an exclusively human experience is defined by the recognition that humans are connected with each other and with a Higher Being eyond self. Many of my connections have come about from ordinary interactions which are always opportune for great connections.

I was in the examination room after the medical assistant finished her preliminary eye exams for any issues related to diabetes, something I do annually. The doctor walked in and introduced himself. We shook hands then he swung his lenses around to peer into my eyes. He briefed me on the pictures and diagrams from the technician.

In a conversational tone, he asked, "where did you grow up?" The question did not surprise since my accent inevitably invites similar questions. So I told him I grew up in Tanzania. "In Arusha?" he asked. "Near Arusha actually", I responded. "Moshi, 50 miles east, on the slopes of Kilimanjaro (my favorite introduction – slopes of Kilimanjaro). Then I asked him, "were you in Arusha?".

Indeed, he was in Arusha for three months and even climbed Kilimanjaro. Our chatting was marked by short sentences and comments because he was concentrating on the examinations which was the purpose of my visit anyway. I managed to let him know that in all likelihood, during his hike on Kilimanjaro he passed by my home village.

This was a very brief encounter, but two complete strangers, for me, in a foreign land, and he at home but also connected to his once foreign land. He got a chance to practice some Kiswahili then we bade each other goodbye. You can call that and similar interactions "chance" but for me they point to human interconnection.

At the end of my first year of graduate school at Hebrew Union College I registered for German lessons in the summer at the University of Cincinnati. During the year I had met and become friends with a German couple I met at the Lutheran Campus Ministry. Naturally I mentioned the fact that I would be studying their language – a requirement, along with French, in graduate studies in Humanities.

When we met again a few days later, Karin was quite excited which was uncommon for a German. She could no wait to share with me some exciting news. "My friend will be your German teacher" she said, "and she said she knows you from Tanzania".

As it turned out, her friend, Ursula, while traveling in Tanzania almost ten years earlier, stayed in our house for a weekend. She was visiting a school for the blind about 100 miles from my home town where I had escorted some German friends and on my way back a friend asked me to look after Ursula who was traveling on the same bus. I accompanied her to her missionary doctor friends near my home town with whom she was going to stay.

She promised to visit the seminary where I was if she should be in the area, and sure enough, a week or two later she came to the seminary and stayed with us for a weekend. Then she went back to Germany and for a while we stayed in touch. Later I went to Jerusalem and she was working with Turkish immigrants in Germany, but gradually we lost contact of each other.

Ten years later, we met again in a Cincinnati classroom, she an instructor of beginners' German and I, a graduate student and now her summer language student. Since then, there have been countless, what I call, Arusha Connections.

Arusha Connections

Within a one-month period I met two strangers with whom a hither-to unknown connection with a faraway small town in a faraway country became the icebreaker into a wonderful conversation and future connection. The small town is Arusha in Tanzania. I have mentioned how, in the course of eye examination, the ophthalmologist and I, two complete strangers, discovered that indeed we have some connection through the small town of Arusha.

Less than a month later, it happened again. This time I accepted to attend a venue – dinner actually – where all the guests, though they knew one another from church, to me they were complete strangers, except the two hosts. By "chance" (here we go again) I was paired with Elizabeth (not her real name).

The idea behind the pairing is to find out through conversation and a few suggested but optional questions, basic relevant information to introduce your partner to the whole group.

"So you are from Tanzania", Elizabeth asked. I answered yes.

"From Arusha?" The same question I was asked a month ago.

"No, actually from Moshi, fifty miles east of Arusha, on the foot of Kilimanjaro" Again, almost word for word, my response to the ophthalmologist.

That set us on to the most uplifting conversation I could ever have imagined. Not only was she in Arusha with World Vision (and my daughter works with World Vision in Arusha) the two of us also have an Israel connection. We shared memories of Mount Scopus, the Lutheran church's Augusta Victoria hospital and World Vision in the same area, Church of the Redeemer in the Old City, the Anglican St. George's College and Christ Church.

But what is most fascinating is that this discovery between Elizabeth and me was a shared experience with all the other pairs. They all have extensive international experience and mindset and they have passion for the church and its mission. Furthermore, even though they know one another from church, the time we spent eating and talking revealed much that turned out to be fresh insight about each one.

The larger picture for me is that we are never strangers from one another. There are no aliens among us. We belong together. It is fear only that separates us and leads us into believing that those we don't know are different from us; that there is in fact "we" and "they"'

Connections Through Affliction

I still remember some sermons of my childhood pastor
when I was growing up on the slopes of Kilimanjaro. They are
sermons that targeted the principle feature of any social
gathering among the Wachaga: pombe, a local brew made from
bananas and millet. Drinking pombe is a tradition that
transcends ages. There are any number of reasons, and none,
why people got together to drink.

As one would expect there were adverse consequences from
this social enterprise, especially economically. For some people
drinking was their main – if not the only occupation. But then,
there were also some who had complete control over their
drinking habits. For this reason, those with no control were
morally weak.

So, it was incumbent upon the weak to straighten up. That
became the theme of many of my pastor's sermons I still
remember. From the pulpit he bellowed:

"There is no house, with starving children, skinny cows,
skinny dogs and skinny cats, like a house governed by alcohol.

There is no house where husband and wife live in more misery than a house governed by alcohol".

We heard these sermons again and again, but nothing changed. Even those who wanted to change, they could not. Why? Because they were morally weak.

Even on a national level, I still remember president Julius Nyerere chastising "walevi na wazururaji" – drunkards and loiterers. I am saying drunkards because that was the term we knew; the designation of alcoholics was unknown. In other words, they were people who drank too much, a moral failure; and it was up to them to change.

There are certain common societal mindsets about different groups or categories of people. In fact specific terms have evolved and become acceptable in defining others. Some examples are, the homeless, the poor, addicts, disabled, and so on. These are stereotypes and as with all stereotypes, they provide a distorted view of the people they are meant to define. As a principle, definitions are not at all helpful or even appropriate.

City Gospel Mission gave me the opportunity to interact with those society has labeled the homeless, the poor, and addicts. Through the recovery program I learned what it means to struggle with addiction of any kind. There are tears shed and attempted suicides. Some even succeed in suicide.

I saw mothers struggle to see their sons through the process to recovery. I'll use pseudonyms here to illustrate a real life example of the anguish that individuals, families and any who are driven by love go through.

Ernest came to the program from the intensive care unit where he lay for three days following a near death experience due to drug overdose. For a Christian, the near death experience was pretty sobering. He had no doubt in his mind that God rescued him from certain death and since everything happens for a purpose, he was resolved to live for that purpose.

At 30, Ernest had a four year old son who he loved dearly. Because of his struggles with drugs, his relationship with his son's mother – they were not married – was so broken it was non-existent. Consequently, Ernest's mother, Eileen, had custody of the little boy

Eileen was a loving mother who wanted the best for her son and grandson. She in fact brought Ernest to the program following his discharge from the hospital.

Ernest believed that God gave him a second chance so that he could live for his son.

Eileen supported Ernest in every possible means towards his recovery. Every weekend, along with her grandson, she came to visit Ernest. The only weekends she missed were due conflicting scheduling with her work or the program. She volunteered for the marathon race so that she, along with other volunteers, could practice and participate in the race to support Ernest and everyone in the recovery program.

After several weeks, while seemingly making progress in the program, Ernest relapsed, for the first time. Relapse is part of the recovery process, so it was not so surprising to those running the program. It was a disappointing experience though for Eileen as it would be for any parent or loved one.

To some Christians though, and given Ernest's divine gift of a second chance, the relapse demonstrated lack of commitment.

After the requisite program requirements following the relapse, Ernest was back on course through recovery. Again, after some weeks he relapsed again. This time, he was ready to throw in the towel. But Eileen's love would not give up. There was a scene on the streets in Over the Rhine as Ernest tried to run away and Eileen chased after him.

"Get back to the program", she called. "You must get back to the program, or you will never see your son again". The scene continued for what must have been a couple of hours. Eventually she caught up with him and through sheer determination – and threats, of course, Ernest was back in the program.

Those leading recovery programs know that relapses happen, inevitably. The warning to anybody in recovery is "walk humbly", don't expect the worst, but know that it can happen to you. It is devastating when it happens, but what is important is to stand up again and keep walking.

I remember this guy, Len, in one AA group who after four years of sobriety had become a respected leader in the group. He always had sound advice, learned from years of drug addiction and now four years clean.

I remember that day after Labor Day when he came to the meeting sobbing. Most of the group had heard the news but he would have to tell it himself. He was shaking as he made the confession. "Last weekend I had nothing to do, mixed up with old friends and ended up using". I asked the guy sitting next to me, 'what happens to him now?'. He said, "he will have to begin with Step One again".

Devastation, humiliation, shame, weakness,, these are some of the emotions that a relapse produces, and all of which one needs to overcome; and victory comes through humility.

There is always the temptation to imagine one has finally won the race. "Victory is mine", was one of several refrains of a song repeated by a group of men in a recovery program. The tenor declares, "I've got victory; victory is mine". After only a few weeks in a recovery program – as I observed at City Gospel Mission, for example, there is pressure for program participants to give testimony. Churches send out invitations for testimony about what God has done. Unfortunately, and unintentionally perhaps, some of these testimonies turn into "what I have done". And, not long after, there is relapse.

Anyway, back to Len's story. After four years of being clean, he was, in many ways, the inspiration of the group. And he lived up to that: Always cheerful and positive, he had a word of encouragement for everyone who showed up in a meeting.

I remember the day he shared his experience taking his son for his first day of school. "It's a miracle", he proudly pointed out. "Me taking my son to his first day of school! Five years ago, this was unthinkable. I would not have even been aware there was a son who needed me. I could not take care of myself, much less my son".

This was a common confession for many – most of them in their 50s - "I never took care of anything, not bills, not kids, not even myself! My mother did that". Len's confession resonated with many in those meetings – as all confession speak to all in recovery. And now, there was a new chapter for Len. Four years clean, taking care not only of himself – and you could see that: Dressed in a grey designer suit, dress-shirt and impeccable tie, he was in all appearance a responsible individual.

Then it happened.

There was dead silence in that meeting room in the undercroft. The usual cigarette smoke was more intense threatening to choke the one hundred or so in attendance. The usual AA gossip had spread the news, what we needed were details. How did it happen?

When Len walked into the room in the company of three equally respectable companions, you could hear a pin drop. It almost seemed solemn. It was the day after Labor day.

There was no doubt that he had been crying, sobbing, actually. There was sadness, melancholy in place of his usual exuberance. "Yesterday", he began, faultily, "I did not have much to do; I ended up using. It was my fault, I mixed up with old friends, which I should have known better, and I fell. I admit my fault and I am determined to stand up again".

After another moment of silence and reflection came the reaction. By and large there were expression of sympathy and soul searching. But there were also expressions of judgment and condemnation. "How could you let yourself off guard?". These were the more severe. "You ought to have known not to hang out with old cronies. That is why we have these meetings", and so on.

Despite his strong posture, you could see his shame and humiliation.

Ed, sitting next to me, and as experienced with AA as Len was stood up to bring the comments to an end. "Moments like these are not times for chastisement and judgment, he said. "Nobody here can answer the question why? That is the nature of addiction and relapse. When it happens it is like being hit by a freight train. There is no preparation and the hindsight is equally baffling". His advice was for everyone to help him move forward, not trying to figure out why.

I thought, perhaps, the experience would prove beneficial on the road of recovery. Saint Teresa of Avila gave us this quote: "To reach something good it is very useful to have gone astray – and thus acquire experience". On the journey to recovery there are failures and disappointments to be encountered, and that is alright. Failure during an endeavor is, in the long run, profitable. The problem is not trying at all.

Even more problematic is the attitude that some have towards people like Len or Eric. People in recovery are simultaneously confronting negative emotions: Shame, guilt, humiliation, lack of trust and so on. Many have been told – because of their experience, perhaps – that they do not measure up. "You are weak! You cannot achieve anything! You are a thief", and so on. These negative emotions create low self-esteem. It is a fact that people with low self-esteem are more likely to sabotage themselves when something good is happening to them – like recovery – because they don't feel deserving.

Each new day in the recovery program began with this recitation: "I am somebody...I love myself...I am somebody". It was a way to begin the day, and a powerful message for those in recovery.

In her book, The Gift of Imperfection: Let go of who you think you're supposed to be and embrace who you are, Brene Brown writes: "If we want to fully experience love and belonging, we must believe that we are worthy of love and belonging". Wanting to be loved, and to love, and to belong is the most powerful force of human life. That is why an addict would want to be clear about.

Bene Brown continues, "When we can let go of what other people think and own our story, we gain access to our worthiness – the feeling that we are enough just as we are and we are worthy of love and belonging. When we spend a lifetime trying to distance ourselves from the parts of our lives that don't fit with who we think we're supposed to be, we stand outside of our story and hustle for our worthiness by constantly performing, perfecting, pleasing and providing. Our sense of worthiness – that critically important piece that gives us access to love and belonging – lives inside of our story".

She continues: "The greatest challenge for most of us is believing that we are worthy now, right this moment. Worthiness doesn't have prerequisites. So many of us have knowingly created/unknowingly allowed/been handed down a long list of worthiness prerequisites:

- I'll be worthy when I lose twenty pounds.

- I'll be worthy if I can get pregnant.

- I'll be worthy if I get/stay sober.

- I'll be worthy if everyone thinks I'm a good parent..."

I wanted to include this detailed quote in full because in recovery, the sense of worthiness is a major struggle. How about the past? The failures? Nothing to show for a lived life? And of course all the negative words from family and peers? Believing to be worthy of anything is a big challenge. For the perfectionist too, but we'll reserve that for fuller discussion later.

Unfortunately, at the earliest taste of the right course or direction pride may take over. Humility that everyone emphasizes as all-important for recovery and sobriety seems to be particularly elusive.

A Long Life with Twists

Palmistry is in the category of pseud-science according to academic experts. Because of varied interpretations in reading palms and also lack of concrete support for the predictions based on the readings science has excluded it from its league. The same can be said about horoscopes and lunar effects on human behavior and the like.

One day, in my youth, a friend persuaded me to accompany him to a palmist. After his reading he convinced to find out what secrets lay in my life as revealed in my palms. It was not a field I was aware of even though palm reading is common in many cultures and is as old as culture itself. Furthermore, along with astrology, it was not only shunned by the church but condemned as un-Christian.

So, when I sat down and gave my left hand to the palmist, it was with a sense of distrust and avoiding anyone ever finding out that I consulted divination. Curiosity ultimately prevailed against rationality.

The palmist took my left hand, gazed at the open palm, looked straight into my eyes before releasing it temporarily and grabbed my right hand and similarly stared at my open palm.

He gave every indication from his look that he read something quite significant.

"Do you see the lines on your hands", he asked gazing straight into my eyes. Of course, I see them every day. "You have long and deep lines. Notice how one line, on both hands, runs from the wrist to the middle of the forefinger and the thumb". I believe he interpreted the line to represent my heart. Because of its prominence, both in depth and length, "it means you will have a long life". Then he pronounced the downside.

"The long lines also have branches which don't run the whole width of your palms. That is an indication of twists and tur

His conclusion, or reading, was that I have a long life full of turns and twists. I could imagine long life, meaning years or time period. But how do you imagine twists and turns? I decided to brush aside from my mind the whole examination and verdict.

A few months later though, still out of curiosity, I opened my palms for another reader, curious as to what I would hear. By some very strange coincidence, I got the same message.

That was more than forty years ago. I am still here today and indeed there have been many turns and twists along the way. My interest is the twists and turns, not predictions or foreknowledge.

When I was growing up (on the slopes of Kilimanjaro) there were still subtle practices of different forms of divination, even among Christians. Among the older generation, there were tendencies to seek answers from local medicine-men when they could not get answers from doctors, for example. A child is sick, his parents take him to the doctor who prescribes some medicines, but the child is not cured. The parents them consult a local medicine-man. The medicine-man finds out that the child's ancestors are displeased because they have been neglected, so the parents offer a goat and the ancestors are satisfied and the child's health is restored.

That is how some Christians vacillated between Christian faith and local traditions. As would be expected, the church stood in strong opposition to Christians seeking to maintain relations with ancestors or the dead. Such Christians faced excommunication.

Palm-reading was obviously a form of divination. Even today, the science community regards it as a pseudo-science. And so too is astrology; and if the church says it is wrong, so it is.

Truthfully, I have not attempted to find out the connection between the palm-readers message and my ongoing life. Ironically today I see a number of tarot and palm reading parlors in places like Georgetown when these are regarded as no more than superstition in Kilimanjaro.

I spent two nights in a shelter at Niagara Falls Gospel Rescue Mission. I checked in there after I was turned back from the Canadian side of the border. The first evening there I had a conversation with the director of the mission after the intake procedure. I tried to briefly give him an account of my life in Cincinnati, my plan to move to Canada and how I was turned back after crossing the border. While I tried to give as brief but complete account as I could I was not surprised when his reaction was: "My wife and I live a very simple life. We've never been outside the country or outside New York state. We are very happy not to have any complications in life". He couldn't have made it clearer. No twists and no turns. No experience on the precipice.

Faith and Intuition

I am in the second year of a move from Cincinnati to Toronto – actually October 2017 marks the beginning of the third year. The flight time between Cincinnati and Toronto is an hour and a half and driving time is seven hours. Yet, because of "complications" as the director at the Niagara Falls shelter would call it, it has been two years and counting.

This is how I got here: The full implications of my immigration status hit me with some surprise when I was robbed. My wallet stolen and along with it my driver's license and social security card. Until then my visa status was D/S which I understood meant "duration of status". I never bothered to know beyond those three words and nobody had ever asked for a document or anything. So, when City Gospel Mission wanted to hire me, they needed a driver's license and a social security card for payroll purposes. Naturally I went to the Social Security office to ask for a replacement of my stolen card and they needed immigration papers, or driver's license. At the BMV office they wanted a birth certificate or immigration papers. In short, to get one, I would need the other and to get the other, I would need – well – the other.

So, City Gospel Mission petitioned for a Religious Worker visa on my behalf. After three filings, each seeking to clarify different questions in the application, it came to a point where I needed to show that I was in the same position (chaplain) for a continuous two year period preceding my application and if part of that period of employment was in the United States, that I was in a legal immigration status.

All along, it was for me to present proof of my status.

When I discussed my predicament with my pastor, he suggested that I move to Canada because, for one, and most people agree with this, Canada is a much more welcoming nation than its southern neighbor; perhaps even the most welcoming nation in the world. Secondly, many agree that the so-called "American Dream" is now to be found in Canada. And on a practical level, my pastor has some connections in Toronto and connections is the most important resource.

It means, to me, that I am seeking to start all over again in a new place. I found spiritual strength is this. I remembered Lee Iacocca's words:

"So, what do we do? Anything. Something. So long as we just don't sit there. If we screw it up, start over. Try something else. If we wait until we've satisfied all the uncertainties it may be too late" Horacio Jones' words similarly inspire me: "Instead of saying, 'I'm damaged, I'm broken, I have trust issues' say, 'I'm healing, I'm rediscovering myself, I'm starting over"

That has always been my ideal in life. There is always room to start over and never be afraid. I chose a departure date: September 16, 2015. That one single decision to move has brought with it opportunities to address and deal with other issues I never addressed before and never thought of addressing. Had I sat down to make things perfect, I would still be where I was. And although I am not where I should have been, I am closer there than I was, or, as it is said, I may not be there yet but I am closer than I was yesterday.

I did not have the money or the documents to fly to Toronto. So I bought a bus ticket to Washington DC with the intention of obtaining Tanzania documents, some of which I had lost. I got an Emergency Travel Document, that can be used to travel to Tanzania, but not to Canada.

In hindsight I can see now that I was irrational. But what other options did I have? Sitting in Cincinnati was no longer an option for me. But there was also something, may be, intuitive that gave me inner assurance that God was moving too.

I strongly believed, and still do, in my heart, that God has plans for everyone. I am not one who takes Jeremiah 29:11 out of context or some blind reassurance. I would have given up hope by now. I am equally opposed to those who program God. Some go as far as to assign a time frame to God acting. "Give God a year", they urge. "Surrender to God just for one year and see if God does not bless you. Pray, 'Lord you promised in your word...' God is faithful to do what God promised".

There is a plan for everyone but not the same path. So, I am not convinced by claims made in testimonies, "If God did this to me, God will do it for you" There are, of course, many blessings for surrender and obedience, .but such blessings are not all wrapped in getting what one wants. When I can confidently be patient, I count it as a blessing.

I also believe that setbacks on one's journey may be inconvenient but are not necessarily negative. Nor can we expect to face no challenges and disappointments on the way.

Actually, what I am talking about here is FAITH as opposed to belief even though often we use the two terms interchangeably. This is a journey of faith.

I began my story with Eric Milner-White's prayer: "Lord God; You have called your servants to ventures of which we cannot see the ending; by paths as yet untrodden; through perils unknown. Give us faith to go out with good courage, not knowing where we go, but only that your hand is leading us and your love supporting us; Through Jesus Christ our Lord".

Every day I must keep reminding myself, what this faith means. What is faith? There are many Christians who like to answer the question reciting Hebrews 11:1, "faith is the substance of things hoped for, the evidence of things not seen". Other translations say, "faith is the reality of what is hoped for, the proof of what is not seen", and still others have, "faith is the assurance of things hoped for, the conviction of things not seen" and so on. None of this helps me much on my daily journey, especially because of the chosen words: conviction and assurance,

This terminology implies the absence of doubt. Thus, Hilda Marie Barton writes in her book, There is No Room for Doubt:

The Just Shall Live by Faith, that "the enemy of faith is doubt. You need to replace doubt for faith. For doubt and faith does not go together. You will have one or the other. There is no room for doubt in faith. To doubt the things of God is sin".

Thank God there are so many churches that carry the name St. Thomas. Frederick Buechner points out, "were there no room for doubt there would be no room for faith either".

It is tempting for me to want to sound like those Phillip Yancey refers to (as he quotes Buechner's observation) as Christians who speak "confidently about matters veiled in mystery whose certitude both frighten and fascinate".

I mean, honestly, imagine asking about faith and Hebrews 11:1 is thrust at you: "Now faith is confidence in what we hope for and assurance about what we do not see", or "Now faith is the substance of things hoped for, the evidence of things not seen" (KJV). For many of us this sounds like some theological jargon at a time when I am trying to see my way through.

The Judeo-Christian father if faith, Abraham, set out to go where he did not know, I mean, he had no clue where he was going. God called him to go where he would find out only when he got there. That is pretty scary. Just pack up and go! Where? Never mind. Just trust that God's hand is guiding us.

It is scary when we want assurances all the details. Faith is taking risk to trust God. It is saying, I am staking my life on this, not because of certainties but because God's faithfulness is worthy of the risk.

Scripture tells us that "the Lord had said to Abram, "Go from your country, your people and your father's household to the land I will show you" (Gen. 12:1;). That is not much for a well-established and wealthy person. He obeyed and so he becomes father of faith. On the way he faced trials and doubts. In Genesis 12: 14ff when they came to Egypt, Abraham convinced his wife that they should lie about their relationship to save their skins – actually to save Abraham's skin. We find a similar story, or duplication of the same story in Genesis 20 when Abraham lies to Abimelek King of Gerar.

He had doubts about God's promise to make his descendants as numerous as the stars or the sand on the beach. And especially since both he and his wife were pretty old. They tried to solve this predicament with Abraham fathering a child, Ishmael, with Hagar, Sarah's maid.

So, this was Abraham who heard God speak to him. We can have an endless discussion about how or what he heard. How did God speak to him? What about today? How is God speaking to us? What are we hearing? Are we supposed to hear anything? Is there a call?

I must confess, I heard a lot that is similar to Abraham's call in my own experience. I set out from Cincinnati following on Abraham's example.

Intuition

Often we equate intuition with gut feeling. Some people may feel or think that gut feeling is irrational and in our age and time we want to assess everything on the scale of reason.

Actually, intuition is a product of experience, what we have learned in life, past patterns and projectile and agency. In other words, intuition can call for immediate action or it may caution for more information before action. It can summon immediate action or deferred action.

Intuition summoned me to act now, not later. I had enough information, and experience to determine that staying in Cincinnati in my present circumstances was the equivalent of non-action. True, there were no assurances of my visa situation changing anytime – sooner or later was not important factor. And of course certainties and assurances are not of much significance.

I consulted with my pastor too, so I followed my intuition. That was God's call for me, like Abraham's, to leave my familiar and comfortable (actually not comfortable) surroundings and "go to the land I will show you". For those like me who are seeking to prevail over perfectionism, intuition can sometimes be sidelined while paralyzed in the quest for a perfect plan.

The real enemy of faith is therefore fear and it is fear that chokes intuition. I followed my intuition and stepped out in faith without certainties or assurances.

We have spent quite some time in our bible study group at St. Mark's wrestling with the concept, especially bearing in mind the Hebrew term, emu-nah, which is active like a verb. We could say, not having faith, but faithing, doing or practicing faith. It is a journey, certainly like my journey. It is not static, not a state of being but doing.

I would like to use Frederick Buechner's wisdom to reflect on faith. "Faith is homesickness. Faith is a lump in the throat.

Faith is less a position on than a movement toward, less a sure thing than a hunch.

Faith is waiting. Faith is journeying through space and through time". As Phillip Yancey remarks in his book, Soul Survivor: How Thirteen Unlikely Mentors Helped My Faith Survive the Church, if someone would ask about my faith, "I'd have to talk about the ups and downs of the years, the dreams".

That is my story too in these pages, and the dream for this book. There are no certainties, no assurances, no guarantees, but hope.

It seems to me that the problem in our quest for assurance is another manifestation of the illusive perfection. Chaplains in emergency shelters and recovery programs at times invite participants to share or give testimony of what God has done or is doing in their lives. It is not uncommon to hear lengthy testimonies of what amounts to "what I am doing for God".

What would prompt an individual to find it convenient to pray loudly, only when everybody is sitting for breakfast? Or why would an individual take ten minutes to relate how he has been serving God during the past thirty years? When I asked a friend these questions he thought these were attempts to conceal struggles an individual is facing.

I don't give testimonies, partly as a result of my theological background, and partly because of my struggle with being judgmental. I see value, and real testimony, in actions rather than words. I am more inclined to visualize Jesus and the parable of the Pharisee and the Publican, or tax collector in Luke 18: 9-14 which may be the opposite of what the person is testifying to.

Still, I have a long way to learn Anton Chekhov's technique of "show, don't tell", especially in my writing, but the best testimony is in action, not words.

Those who talk about themselves do a major disservice to testimony and the intended praise of God. People have an inherent abhorrence for self-praise, even in ordinary social gatherings. Instead of the audience praising God people are left with questions about the speaker who they see as boastful and arrogant.

The claim that "if God can do this to me, God will do it to you too" is misleading and often loaded with self-praise. This is a significant temptation for people in recovery programs testifying to people not in a program. I have heard, many times, "I did it; you can do it too!" And if "you are not doing it", it is because you don't have Jesus.

I was a volunteer during the seven years at City Gospel Mission, meaning I did not earn wages nor build up a savings fund. I was empty materially. I was rich though spiritually and I learned to look with gratitude at that side of my life. One of those riches is meaningful relationships.

Until the week of my planned departure I did not know and I did not worry about any details of the journey. I said to myself, I would worry about that when I got to Toronto, not before. My mind was filled with this saying: "The past is your lesson. The present is your gift. The future is your motivation". I am everyday motivated by what lies ahead, the dream.

My pastor, who inspired in me motivation to look beyond my present setbacks of immigration issues, and look into possibilities ahead, in a different place and environment, bought me the bus ticket and gave me one hundred dollars. Two days before my departure, a friend from the bible study group took me to his bank, got me travelers card with five hundred Canadian dollars and a debit card for five hundred US dollars.

When I kept wondering what I did to deserve this generosity he finally helped me out. "It is grace", he told me, "you did not deserve it. How about it, does it help?" Indeed, it was pure grace. Out of the blue, he said I had been unselfish in the bible study and in my volunteering. Not once had I given any thought to my volunteer work or whatever input I had in our bible study group. This friend would go on to bless me with a total of almost two thousand dollars towards my dream.

There were others too who I am not listing here who came to my assistance financially. It was the most tangible manifestation to me, that God is working on my behalf. And how can I take those positive developments and not the setbacks? I choose to remind myself constantly, that "all things work together for good to those who love God" (Romans 8:28). All things must include setbacks.

That has been my mindset.

Everything seemed to work smoothly, even the weekend I spent in Washington DC. I got an Emergency Travel Document from the Tanzania embassy, one of the other priests at my now former parish paid for my hotel and on Monday I resumed my journey. We had a long stopover in Buffalo, New York and when they called for boarding for the Toronto bus the whole line was of Asians and Hispanic. The driver went down the line looking at passports and visa stamps. When he came to me I gave him my travel document.

He looked at it then asked, "what is this?" I told him what it was. He went to the office with the document and returned momentarily and handed it back to me. "I can't take you", he told me. I pleaded with him to take me to the border. "I can't take you", he repeated. "You can take a taxi". And that is exactly what I did.

The taxi drivers consulted among themselves and agreed that there was no way they could take me across the river but they could take me to the pedestrian bridge and let me walk across to the Canadian side. There was nobody on the US side of the border, so I walked through the revolving gate, pulling my luggage, and emerged on the other side and onto the bridge.

I heard the roaring as the water dropped down Niagara Falls. White mist rose from the water falls and extended high into the sky. Gradually the falls came into full view to the west and I took a few minutes to snap some pictures. From where I was the falls did not look like anything you see on postcards. There was no sign of tourists, not on my bridge or anywhere around. Actually I did not meet anyone all along the bridge.

It was late September – the 21st actually - around ten in the morning. According to the bus schedule I had chosen, I intended to be in Toronto in the morning or afternoon, certainly not in the evening or at night.

It felt very fresh on the bridge. The sky was clear and blue, the air fresh and thin. Most people in Cincinnati wondered about the timing for my move to Toronto noting that at this time of the year people ordinarily go south and I was heading in the opposite direction. I never gave any rationale then for the timing but on reflection I realize that most of my moving have been mostly in July.

Anyway, my first encounter with a Canadian border official was this rather very young lady who seemed to be all along when I entered the border post. She was extremely polite as I explained to her that I was literally fleeing the US because I had been most miserable.

She listened with clear sympathy on her face. She looked at my Emergency Travel Document then directed me to cross over what looked like a trench to another part of the border post where another officer stood examining my movement. He was also young, may be late twenties early thirties and looked very professional and confident.

He asked if I had any weapons in my suitcase or anything like that and if I had any money. I answered no to the first and yes to the second question. He told me to open my suitcase, keep the money and wallet then he showed me where to put the luggage. As he was looking at my travel document, I tried the best I could to present my case and to present the human face behind the story.

I told him that because of politics, what I referred tas politics of immigration, I felt my hands tied in the US, with no other option but to leave and start life again somewhere else – in Canada, specifically.

"What politics", he remarked with a tinge of retort in his voice. "There is politics here in Canada too".

It did not sound too reassuring to me. First, I had been encouraged with the new administration of a liberal party which seemed to want to reverse the hardline policies of the previous conservative administration. The new prime minister had sent a message to the world that "we have not forgotten you and that Canada would be a place of compassion again". There was a general sense that Canada was going to continue to be a land of hope for immigrants, foreigners, an international community, a distinction that had gradually been eroded during the previous eight years.

The second encouragement was information I found on the internet claiming that the border officials could permit entry into Canada on individual basis. In fact the website advised being truthful and every respect; in responding to questions asked and, in presenting your case. I have always believed that the truth always wins in the end and so the website reinforced my confidence.

We went into an examination room. It was a large room with benches and large windows which made me think it was not a detention room or anything like that. There was only one door and although the officer left the room for long periods, the door remained open. Again, I was the only person in there for the six hours or so that I was there.

Since I mentioned that I had diabetes medications in my suitcase around noon the officer asked me what I would like to eat since he was going to order something for. I was not feeling hungry but he insisted that he order something, so I accepted a soda.

During the interrogation he asked if I had any relatives in Canada, whether I would apply for permanent residence, if I would seek long term employment or short-term and so forth. I answered as truthfully as I knew the truth at that moment. Then, suddenly he asked me if I would like to apply for asylum.

The question jolted me and I thought he saw the shock in my eyes. An asylum? It had never occurred to me. I was not fleeing persecution even though US immigration stalemate had reduced me to the predicament of a refugee. Ironically too, deep inside me, I was fleeing some form of injustice.

All my life I saw myself as an internationalist, or a citizen of the world. Very rarely do I carry a mindset of locality.

Ironically too, most Americans living overseas or those who have traveled overseas have an internationalist mindset.

In Jerusalem my American friends and I were impressed to observe that most of us were tuned to BBC World Service as our morning rise up alarm. BBC World Service was a symbol of international mindset.

"I'm trying to advise you..." he started, then caught himself and stopped. "I'm trying to give you information as to what is possible, and what is not. I mean, it's up to you. If you want to file an application for asylum". Even though it had never crossed my mind that I could ask for asylum anytime or anywhere, at this particular moment what I needed was entry into Canada. Everything else would follow from there and as to what everything else could be, I had not figured that out.

My first order of business when I got to Toronto would be to find a place to stay – may be in a setting similar to City Gospel Mission where I could also serve in some kind of ministry. I had gathered some information about Sanctuary Toronto from someone who lived in that community and I had also been in contact with the executive director to explore possibilities of residence there. My pastor too, who had supported my vision gave me a contact, a friend who is very familiar with Toronto and Canada in general and the church. That is all I had in my vision.

But now the officer said he was giving me valuable information about available possibilities. I have to note here with special emphasis that he was not a lawyer – not my lawyer even if he could have been a lawyer by training. Whatever valuable information he purported to give me and my acceptance of it turned out to be a big mistake, but I had no way of knowing then. It would have been better to have left it alone.

But I took his "advice-later-corrected-to-offer-of-valuable-information". I don't know exactly how long it took. It was quite a long time. There were moments when the officer would leave me in the room for a while while he disappeared, they he would come back and continue with the interview, then leave, then come back again and so on.

I still remember some of the questions: Did I have relatives in Canada? Am I a native Indian? Was I looking for full time job? Was I seeking permanent residence or temporary stay? I had resolved, from the beginning, that I was going to appeal my case to the border personnel and lay out my story as clearly and truthfully as possible. And that was what I did.

Then he left the room again for what felt like quite a long time. I sat there in the room, staring at the wall, my mind blank as I cannot recall anything going on in my mind. Then another officer came in.

He greeted me, then introduced himself. He read back to me the interview I had with the other officer and asked me if everything was correct. I said it was. He went on to inform me of the protocol for asylum applications and admittance. An officer makes a recommendation which is reviewed by a superior officer and if both of them agree on the recommendation (for admission) then the application goes to a judge.

He told me that the officer did not recommend that my application qualified to go before a judge and he, as the superior officer agreed with him. Therefore, he said, "you must return to the United States at the earliest, and if you do not comply you will be arrested and deported". It turned out that I should not have accepted the officer's "advice or valuable information" to apply for asylum. I could not apply for asylum from the United States because I have no rights there.

Anyway, they transported me to the U.S border patrol office where I spent, may be four hours or so. The officers there went through their data records, I answered questions, they double-checked, then they said they had nothing on record against me. They asked if I had any money for hotel and I answered that I had only $300 to my name and I would not spend it for a one-night hotel room. They took me to a shelter and the following morning I found Niagara Falls Gospel Rescue Mission where I stayed for a couple of days.

During the interview at the Canadian border I learned some important lessons. I don't have relatives in Canada, but as I told the officers, I'll need connections. It's scary not to have relatives when contemplating moving to a new place. But connections are as good as relatives and we are wired to connect. When the officers dropped me at the shelter they were essentially saying to me, "buddy, you are on your own". Actually, that's what it means when you are told, "good luck to you". It can be scary too to imagine being alone. But I have learned also that we are not alone.

Being Open-Minded

There are things or events that tend to leave lasting impression in mind. My first day in the Men's Bible Study at Christ Church Cathedral will always be memorable to me. Looking back at the time I see why the group was such a supportive community for us. From there I have come to appreciate the value of groups like where one feels to belong.

I had been going to Christ Church Cathedral for a couple of years, mainly to the noon Eucharist on Wednesdays and Fridays. That is how I got to know Christ Church Cathedral. With my weekend outreach ministry at City Gospel Mission I missed Sunday worship services, and Holy Communion in particular.

So, I was intentionally looking for a church that has weekday Eucharist. And so I stumbled into Christ Church Cathedral one Wednesday after I saw on the bulletin board outside the church that they had Wednesday and Friday noon Eucharist.

At that time my head was full of negative things said and written about the Episcopal church. In fact, for almost two to three years prior I had absorbed much of it into my head mostly because I just relished a church being ridiculed, especially by dissidents from within. To say the least I did not know how I would feel inside that chapel where the noon Eucharist was celebrated.

It was a short service, lasting about 40 minutes. There were three or four of us in the pews, the same people who attended that service regularly. In due time we too became buddies.

I liked the liturgy – very much. Somehow, the liturgy of the church has always been my main attraction. I know some people are drawn to a particular church because of sermons, music and so on. My attraction is liturgy. During that Wednesday noon Eucharist I discovered the beauty of the liturgy of the Episcopal church and because of that, I fell in love with the Episcopal church.

After the service, as we were heading to the door, the priest rushed to the door as if to corner me. She asked if I was new or I worked in town. I introduced myself and told her what brought me to the noon service. She invited me to come back and pointed out that there was also a Friday noon Eucharist. Then we parted.

Like many, including Episcopalians, I carried the impression that Episcopalians are – as they say – "stand offish". It appeared as though the priest was not particularly pushy to get my e-mail or to sign up a visitor register or anything like that I was not surprised when she did not urge me, "please do come back again", she simply said, "you are most welcome here" and walked away.

I went back on Friday and there was another priest and the same ritual for a newcomer. She spent more time to give me information about other regular activities of the parish: Community Issues Forum on alternate Thursdays when during lunch break the cathedral facilitates discussions of issues of the city and community in general, the Tuesday lunchtime music offerings, Lenten and Advent lecture series, to mention just a few.

There was a lot more than noon Eucharist, most of which appealed to my taste. One day, after noon Eucharist, I was talking to one of the priests when she mentioned that there was actually a Men's Bible Study group that met on Thursday morning. I decided to check it out.

The group met in the library from 8 to 9 and strictly adhered to the time. There is commitment because most in the group have to go to work. What we knew was that the one hour was almost sacred time. Whatever daily commitments we had, we did not schedule anything on Thursday from 8 to 9.

So, on my first day I walked into the library and there were these seven men. Altogether there were about 12 men in the group but seven or eight attended regularly. They welcomed me – it was still coffee time, so I got myself a cup. The spokesperson, Ben (not his real name) introduced those present; three retirees, two self-employed business owners, an employee of the cathedral, one unemployed and the leader of the group, a former Roman Catholic priest.

Even before Ben introduced the former priest I thought he looked like a priest. It is one of those strange phenomenon where some people look like their profession. I have always had a hunch for picking out the clergy in a gathering when everybody is incognito. I can pretty easily pick out a Roman priest – and I mean without the Roman collar.

After the introductions Ben gave me a brief history of the group and their agreed regulations: During the discussion, be considerate of others, give everyone a chance to speak and don't interrupt a speaker. Be courteous when responding to another person's point of view. Most importantly, "anything spoken here remains here".

There is a good reason for the last rule. Fred (not his real name) was a jokester who could abruptly and without notice, crack a joke which probably would best not be shared outside the group. Yes, laughter was an important part of the bible study.

The format was a discussion of the following Sunday's readings from the Lectionary with the intention to guess – at best – what the preacher's sermon will be like. In the days when a member of the clergy participated in the bible study (at this time the cathedral had one male and four female clergy, with the females disqualified from the men's group – just kidding, of course) it was a useful resource for sermons.

We started with the Collect than went around everyone reading a paragraph. When we came to the Gospel Reading which happened to be the parable of the talents, the former priest was reading the paragraph where the servant who was given one talent decided to bury it in the ground until the master returned.

This is how the priest read it – which is why it made a lasting impression in my mind: "He also who had received the one talent came forward saying, "Master, I knew you to be a hard man, reaping where you did not sow, and gathering where you scattered no seed, so I was afraid and went and hid your talent in the ground. Here. You have what is yours. But his master answered him, "You, son of a bitch…"

All of us burst out in laughter. It was my first day of bible study and I said to myself, "this is what bible study should be. We should be able to laugh".

I went to Christ Church Cathedral for two years or so,. We had great camaraderie in bible study and in noon Eucharist. We became friends. Nobody once asked me if I wanted to become a member of the parish or the Episcopal church. But there was no doubt in my mind. That was the church I wanted.. I knew I was loved, I was connected, I belonged. I fell in love with the Episcopal church and I have continued to love the church.

Having fun was an important benefit of bible study. Our resident jokester did not fail us. Like Jews, Episcopalians like to make fun of themselves. This is one of my favorites jokes: Down the street from the Methodist church there lived a single mother with her three young kids. She never went to church even though it was so close. So, one Sunday morning, after service, the pastor decided to visit her and invite her to church. She told the pastor that she and her kids had not been to church because they did not have clothes for church. The pastor said that was not a problem so he went and talked to the women of his church. They said it was not a problem, so they went and bought clothes for the lady and her kids. The following Sunday everybody was feeling so good as they expected to see the woman and her kids in church. But they did not show up. So, after church the pastor went down the street to visit her and find out what could have been the problem this time.

"Oh, no! There is no problem at all", said the woman, with excitement in her voice. "The clothes were so good. When we put them on, we looked so good, we decided to go to the Episcopal church".

This relaxed fellowship full of laughter and humor kept us wanting more and more. One member used to say – at least when the priest was not in attendance – that he got more from bible study than the sermon on Sunday.

The first thing I did when I got to Buffalo was to find a bible study group. I found one that met on Wednesdays during lunch break, in the parish house of St. Paul Cathedral. There were eight in attendance on my first Wednesday. According to the group leader, there were twelve regular attendees.

This was a truly ecumenical group but my friends in Cincinnati thought it was strange that the group met in the Episcopal parish house and the bible study was listed in the Sunday bulletins but there was no Episcopalian in the group.

Anyway, on that Wednesday, and I attended only twice, the group leader reiterated the need for accountability. "Fellowship and accountability", as he put. After work, he was going to call all those who did not communicate anything about their absence. "Fellowship and accountability", he repeated.

Unlike our group at Christ Church Cathedral which was informal by intention, this one required extensive preparation. The leader, or the group as a whole. Chose a topic or book of the bible and assigned to one person to prepare and lead a discussion.

Since then I have joined another group at St. Mark Episcopal church which meets Wednesdays from 11 to 12:15. It is one of three groups at St. Mark. Most of its members are retirees, men and women. The average age is mid-seventies with three ladies in late nineties. Some have been in the group for 60 years or more. For most, the group is like family.

It is a fellowship where we meet to discuss an assigned reading (usually a theological book). The group is intellectually talented and some of the issues we discuss are quite complex.

The emphasis, despite the reading and discussion is fellowship. After bible study we spend more time eating brown bag lunch and share whatever ideas one may have. Like the men's group, here too some express the significance of this

fellowship in their daily life – it is more than the Sunday
service.

Your Elevation May Require Your Isolation

I have, on many occasions, taken the "spiritual gifts test"
hoping to discover what my spiritual gifts are. In the course of
teaching classes on Paul's epistle to the Romans, when we got
to chapter 12 I got everyone to do the test to see how they have
been gifted in the seven spiritual gifts variously described as
prophecy, ministry or serving, teaching, exhortation, or
encouraging, giving, leading, and mercy, or compassion.

I have gone into these self-tests expecting teaching to come
up on top, primarily because my students and colleagues
believe teaching to be my talent. But it never on top. Every
time I take the test, compassion turns out on top. But then,
could this not be the way I would like to see myself? I want to
be kind and compassionate and I am aware too that there are
times when I can be judgmental – not quite mean-spirited or

harsh but perhaps not wanting to be bothered or to go the extra mile. Even in those times though, it bothers my conscience and I want to show kindness.

After almost seven years at City Gospel Mission and I made the decision to move on, there was this tradition of co-workers coming together for lunch and farewell. I invited a few friends from Christ Church Cathedral, who, to my total surprise showed up, some at very short notice.

The president of the Mission spoke for a few minutes and I was equally surprised that his speech was entirely about Joel's humility. Citing my background he contrasted that with how during the seven years or so I accepted with enthusiasm to be in ministry and to live with people living on the precipice, entirely as a volunteer at the Mission and as chaplain at Crossroad Health Center.

I could not claim to be humble, because then it wouldn't be humility. But I saw it as a blessing for which I am grateful that others would see that in me. In fact I found out that the reason those guests showed up at such short notice was in my honor.

Who wouldn't be encouraged to know people are appreciative even if they don't always say so?

These are things I learned through experience living on the precipice. Without the experience, I would be clueless. But the experience makes me more appreciative of life and that situations and circumstances don't diminish us. On the contrary we are better because of trying experiences like life on the precipice.